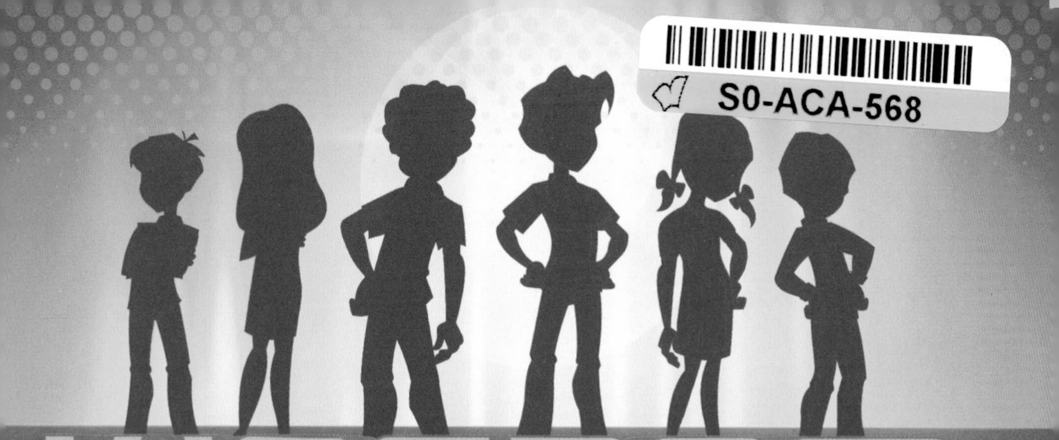

KINGDOM QUEST

TAKING FAITH AND CHARACTER TO THE NEXT LEVEL

AGES 7–10 A STRATEGY GUIDE FOR KIDS AND THEIR PARENTS/MENTORS

TONY EVANS

author of *Raising Kingdom Kids*

Tyndale House Publishers, Inc.
Carol Stream, Illinois

You will have complete and free access to God's kingdom, keys to open any and every door: no more barriers between heaven and earth, earth and heaven.

Matthew 16:19, MSG

Kingdom Quest: A Strategy Guide for Kids and Their Parents/Mentors

A Focus on the Family book published by Tyndale House Publishers, Inc., Carol Stream, Illinois 60188

Editor: Marianne Hering

Cover design by Troy Black

Interior design by Nicole Grimes

Cataloging in Publication Data for this title is available at www.loc.gov.

ISBN 978-1-58997-807-2

For manufacturing information regarding this product, please call 1-800-323-9400.

For information about special discounts for bulk purchases, please contact Tyndale House Publishers at csresponse@tyndale.com, or call 1-800-323-9400.

Printed in China

24 23 22 21 20 19 18
9 8 7 6 5 4 3

CONTENTS

A NOTE FROM DR. TONY EVANS

Are you ready for a quest to discover more about yourself? The first things you'll find out are these:

- You are unique.
- You have a purpose.
- You have a path to take.

This *Kingdom Quest* strategy guide will help you be the strongest, smartest, wisest, and best *you* that you can be. Inside you'll find some tips, truths, and tools to plan your life. It will help you discover more about who you are, who God is, and how you can go further in life than you ever thought possible.

I encourage you to open your heart to what God may reveal through these pages. Make a commitment to finish the guide, and have fun in the process! (Make sure your parents and/or mentors—we call them *Guides* throughout this book—download the *Kingdom Quest Parent/Mentor Guide* at RaisingKingdomKids.org/parenting-tools.)

You have potential for a promising future, and I want to help you get there!

Tony Evans

AN INTRODUCTION TO KINGS AND KINGDOMS

One day Jesus' friends asked Him who was the greatest in His kingdom. Jesus answered in an amazing way. He pointed out a nearby kid and said, "He is."

Jesus said the person who is the greatest is like a kid: trusting and full of faith.

If you're young, Jesus says you're great in His kingdom. You already have a head start on the rest of us. In fact, His kingdom is made up of people, called *subjects*, just like *you*!

What else is Jesus' kingdom like? Well, it's an unusual kingdom. It's one without borders and time. The rules of this earth don't apply there. It has its own rules, weapons, wisdom, and purpose. For example, in Jesus' kingdom it doesn't matter what color your skin is or if you're a boy or a girl.

Power goes to the weak in Jesus' kingdom—that's opposite of the way it is on earth. The weak subjects depend on God and His strength, and He gives them power.

In this kingdom, like in all kingdoms, there is a vile enemy. Satan, the enemy leader, seeks to dethrone the King. Satan also seeks to destroy *you*. He is attempting to pull as many subjects away from the King's rule as possible.

How does Satan do this? He will use a lot of tricks. Some of them are charm, deception, temptation, and pride. He also wants to establish a rival kingdom where evil is practiced instead of the good principles of the King.

So it's all about *you*. Jesus wants *you* to stop Satan's plans. Your mission is to advance the King's rule on earth. You need to use the weapons of warfare to resist and defeat the enemy.

Your task won't be easy, but it will be worth it. Go.

WEAPONS OF WARFARE

In God's kingdom, every subject is a soldier. You must know how to use the weapons God has entrusted to you as His soldier. Ephesians 6:11–17 shows you how to be ready for battle:

> Put on all of God's armor. Then you can stand firm against the devil's evil plans. Our fight is not against human beings. It is against the rulers, the authorities and the powers of this dark world. It is against the spiritual forces of evil in the heavenly world.
>
> So put on all of God's armor. Evil days will come. But you will be able to stand up to anything. And after you have done everything you can, you will still be standing.
>
> So remain strong in the faith. Put the belt of truth around your waist. Put the armor of godliness on your chest. Wear on your feet what will prepare you to tell the good news of peace. Also, pick up the shield of faith. With it you can put out all of the flaming arrows of the evil one. Put on the helmet of salvation. And take the sword of the Holy Spirit. The sword is God's word.

There are six pieces of armor described in Ephesians. They can be divided into two groups. The first group contains three pieces of the armor. You should wear these pieces all of the time. You should never take them off. Think of them like a uniform a baseball player puts on when he goes out to play. The player wears the uniform the entire time he is in the game.

The three pieces in the second group are weapons to pick up as you need them. Ephesians tells you to "put on" these pieces. This is like that same baseball player grabbing his glove or his bat, depending upon where he is in the game.

CATEGORY 1: PIECES TO WEAR ALL THE TIME

In Jesus' kingdom, the subjects are expected to wear and use these pieces of armor given to them. The three pieces to be worn at all times during battle are

- **a belt**
- **armor on your chest**
- **shoes**

THE BELT OF TRUTH

A Roman soldier's belt was used to hold his weapons. The belt held his sword, a dagger, and any other items he needed. He was prepared for battle.

A belt also kept a soldier from falling. How? Well, part of a soldier's uniform was a long tunic. The tunic might trip him during battle, and so the soldier needed to keep it away from his feet. He would pick up the bottom part of the tunic and tuck it into his belt. That way he would not trip on the tunic.

The leather belt kept the Roman soldier prepared and standing. That's a lot like a spiritual belt of truth. A spiritual belt keeps a Christian mentally prepared for battle. It also keeps him or her standing on God's Word. Jesus' soldiers will be able to remain steady and loyal when Satan comes to attack.

THE ARMOR OF GODLINESS

The belt of truth comes first because truth is the foundation for our actions. We first must *know* what is right (truth) before we can *do* what is right. A godly person does what is right, and he or she needs the armor of godliness. This piece is also called the "breastplate of righteousness." A *breastplate* protects a person's heart and lungs. *Righteousness* simply means "being or doing what is right." This piece of armor protects us from Satan's attacks. But it also allows us to push into enemy territory and do good works for the kingdom.

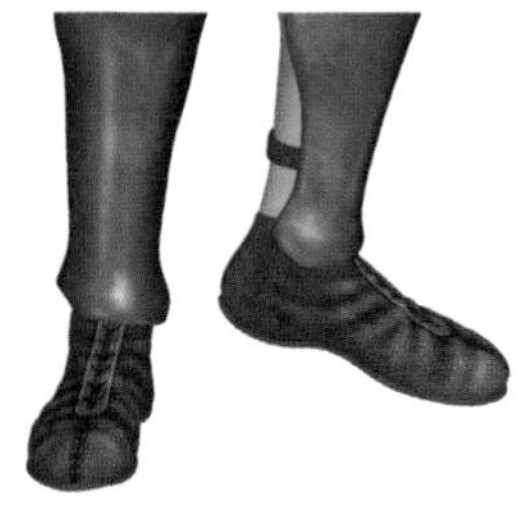

SHOES OF PEACE

A Roman soldier's sandals had short, fat nails called *hobnails*. These hobnails were put through the sole of the shoe. Hobnails were similar to cleats in the shoes worn by football and soccer players. Hobnails gave the sandals traction and kept the soldier from slipping and sliding. It gave him sure footing so he could move quickly in battle. The hobnails made it more difficult for someone to knock down the soldier.

When you wear your shoes of peace, it creates traction. If you have traction, Satan can't knock you off of your feet. A peaceful person is stable, calm, and at rest within. If a person is not at peace, he or she has inner chaos and worry.

CATEGORY 2: PIECES TO PICK UP AND USE AS NEEDED

The following pieces of armor are to be used when needed:

- **shield of faith**
- **helmet of salvation**
- **sword of the Spirit**

SHIELD OF FAITH

A Roman soldier's shield was four feet long and a little more than two feet wide. A soldier hid underneath the shield when arrows were shot at him.

You can compare this shield to a space capsule's shield. When a space capsule heads home, it needs protection coming into Earth's atmosphere. The heat is so high during reentry that a space capsule—and everyone inside it—would burn up in seconds without a shield. Flames and smoke can engulf the entire capsule, but the shield keeps everything on the inside from being damaged.

Satan seeks to surround you with an atmosphere of chaos and destruction. Taking up your faith shield protects you from those evil forces.

HELMET OF SALVATION

The main purpose of a helmet—in battle, sports, or even in risky situations like construction—is to protect the head from injury to the brain. The brain must be protected because it's made of soft tissue. Once the brain becomes damaged, body functions also become damaged. A football player wears a padded helmet to help absorb the shock when his head gets hit. An athlete with a severe head injury can no longer play at the level he or she once could. In fact, an athlete with a head injury may not even be able to play at all.

The brain is the control center of the body. The mind must be protected with a helmet that is able to absorb the shocks of being hit by the enemy.

SWORD OF THE SPIRIT

This piece of armor is the only weapon used for attacks. The other pieces are designed to hold you steady or protect you against the enemy's schemes. After God outfits you for battle, He gives you an additional weapon with which you can advance. This weapon is the sword of the Spirit—the Word of God.

A Roman soldier had two different types of swords, a long one and a short one. The longer sword had a three-foot-long blade. (That's about the length of a wrapping-paper tube.) It was used to fight an enemy at arm's length. The shorter sword had an eighteen-inch blade. A soldier would use this in close combat situations.

Let's review part of the Ephesians 6 passage. Verse 17 says, "Take the sword of the Holy Spirit. The sword is God's word." When the Scripture instructs us to "take the sword," it is referring to the short sword. The sword of the Spirit is to save you when personal attacks come close to you.

In the battle of life, sometimes it seems as if the enemy is right in your face. Imagine two basketball players. One is shooting and the opponent is trying to block the shot. The blocker will often put his hands in the shooter's face. The shooter will not be able to see the basket. Satan doesn't want us to shoot the ball into the basket. He brings his battle as close to you as possible. This attack can affect your mind, will, emotions, and body. The sword of the Spirit is designed to ward off attacks that are "in your face."

HEROES IN THE HALL OF FAITH

Grab your Bible. Look up the verses in the left-hand column. Find out which Bible hero the passage describes. Draw a line from the Bible verse to the corresponding hero. The first one is done for you.

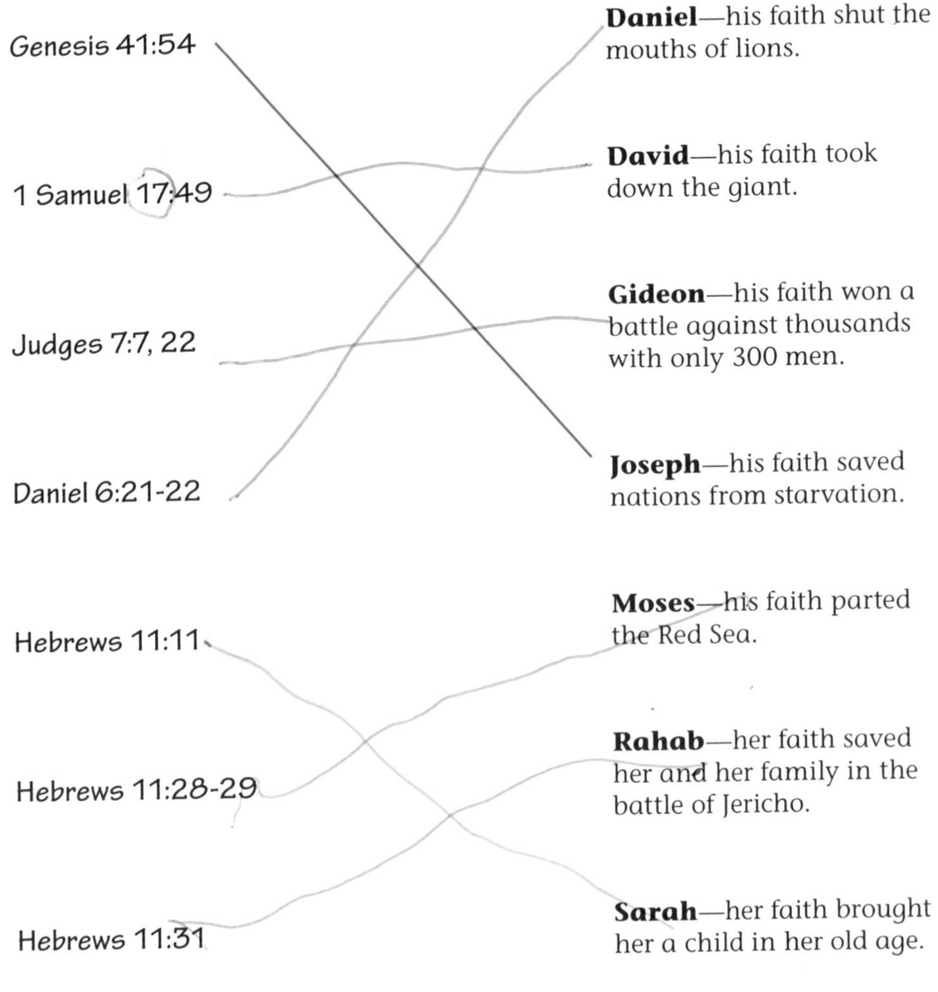

FELLOW SOLDIERS

In Jesus' kingdom, the soldiers are expected to work as a team. Who is doing the *Kingdom Quest* experience with you? Write their names on the following lines. Include your Guide (parent, coach, youth pastor, or mentor) on the list.

Jaida Mom

Dad Me

LEVEL I
MY FORM

MEANING

The traits of a person that make him or her rare, unique, and valuable

IDENTITY

- **UNIQUE**—very special, being unlike any other
- **RARE**—having great value; very few
- **VALUABLE**—of great use and importance

Application: You know that God views you as a one-of-a-kind masterpiece. Masterpieces are rare and valuable.

FROM THE WORD

We are God's creation. He created us to belong to Christ Jesus. Now we can do good works. Long ago God prepared these works for us to do.
—Ephesians 2:10

But God chose you to be his people. . . . You are God's special treasure. You are all these things so that you can give him praise. **—I Peter 2:9**

DEFINE

What does "identity" mean to you?

Identiy means things about a person that are unique, rare and valuable.

QUESTIONS 2 PONDER

1. What three words would you use to describe yourself?

   Smart, funny, likes cooking

2. How do you know who your friends really are? Do you choose friends based on what they say about themselves? Or do you choose them by what they do?

3. Imagine you will be stuck in a room alone for a week. (Yes, you have food, water, clothing, and access to a bathroom.) What four items would you take with you? Why did you choose those items?

   Book dog
   ipad Switch

JUST 4 FUN

Create your identity logo and tagline using the following guide.

1. Draw a personal logo. Make sure it reflects who you are as a person. For example, are you strong? Quiet? Solid? Prone to daydreaming? Here are some ideas:

   - Use colors that reflect your overall personality. For example, yellow could represent someone who is happy and warm.

JUST 4 FUN (CONTINUED)

- The shape and thickness of any letters you use can represent your personality—a thin, fancy letter would show something different than a thick block letter.
- Consider putting your logo inside a "container" such as a square or an oval border.

2. After your logo is finished, develop a tagline. A tagline is a short, creative statement that lets others know who you are. Some sample taglines are:
   - Nike—*Just Do It!*
   - Apple—*Think different*
   - M&M's—*Melts in your mouth, not in your hand*

focused - eyes
silly - mouth

DRAW YOUR LOGO HERE

Beast on the court, beast in the classroom

HERE 2 HELP

Have you ever licked out of a bowl that was used for cookie batter? I think you have! But have you ever grabbed the baking soda and put some into your mouth?

I doubt it. Baking soda is bitter.

But after all the ingredients are mixed together, the batter tastes sweet. After the cookies are baked, they are really good.

In a way, those cookies are just like you. You are a wonderful mixture of your background, talents, hobbies, personality, and more. Sure, some of the "ingredients" of your life have been bitter. Your family may have had some hard times. But God has a way of mixing everything together and turning it into a special you.

A healthy identity form recognizes the God-given strengths of the person. Maybe you are good with numbers, people, music, art, or sports. Be sure to include your strengths on your identity form.

IT'S UP 2 YOU

Read each statement. Then select the response that best reflects the way you think and feel. Next circle the letter next to the answer. Follow the directions on tallying your score at the end of the quiz. Ask your Guide for help if you have questions.

1. I remember that God created me *on* purpose.
   - A. ALWAYS
   - B. MOST OF THE TIME
   - C. SOMETIMES
   - D. NO, I AM NOT SURE.

2. I remember that God created me *for* a purpose.
   - A. ALWAYS
   - B. MOST OF THE TIME
   - C. SOMETIMES
   - D. NEVER

IT'S UP 2 YOU (CONTINUED)

3. I feel good about myself only when I do well in school, in sports, in music, or in another activity.
   A. ALWAYS
   B. MOST OF THE TIME
   C. SELDOM
   D. NEVER

4. I tend to feel worthless because I'm not very good at anything.
   A. ALWAYS
   B. MOST OF THE TIME
   C. SELDOM
   D. NEVER

5. I feel like I am important to my parents and/or other adults in my life.
   A. ALWAYS
   B. MOST OF THE TIME
   C. SELDOM
   D. NEVER

6. I am comfortable being myself around people who are different from me.
   A. ALWAYS
   B. MOST OF THE TIME
   C. SELDOM
   D. NEVER

7. If I got a *really* bad haircut . . .
   A. THE WHOLE SCHOOL COULD MAKE FUN OF ME, AND I WOULDN'T CARE.
   B. IF PEOPLE MADE FUN OF ME, I MIGHT FEEL LIKE CRYING.
   C. I WOULD WEAR A HAT OR ASK MY FRIENDS TO HELP HIDE ME AT LUNCHTIME.
   D. I WOULD TRY TO STAY HOME SO NO ONE WOULD SEE ME, NOT EVEN MY FRIENDS.

8. I can discuss my strengths and weaknesses with others.
   A. YES, WITH MOST PEOPLE
   B. YES, WITH SOME PEOPLE
   C. NOT REALLY
   D. I DON'T KNOW WHAT MY STRENGTHS AND WEAKNESSES ARE.

9. I think most people would reject me if they knew what I am really like.
   A. ALWAYS
   B. MOST OF THE TIME
   C. SELDOM
   D. NEVER

10. I tend to wonder if I will go to heaven when I die.
   A. ALWAYS
   B. MOST OF THE TIME
   C. SELDOM
   D. NEVER

IDENTITY SCORECARD

1. Answer:	A-5	B-4	C-3	D-2	POINTS:
2. Answer:	A-5	B-4	C-3	D-2	POINTS:
3. Answer:	A-2	B-3	C-4	D-5	POINTS:
4. Answer:	A-2	B-3	C-4	D-5	POINTS:
5. Answer:	A-5	B-4	C-3	D-2	POINTS:
6. Answer:	A-5	B-4	C-3	D-2	POINTS:
7. Answer:	A-5	B-4	C-3	D-2	POINTS:
8. Answer:	A-5	B-4	C-3	D-2	POINTS:
9. Answer:	A-2	B-3	C-4	D-5	POINTS:
10. Answer:	A-2	B-3	C-4	D-5	POINTS:

TOTAL POINTS: 

IT'S UP 2 YOU (CONTINUED)

IDENTITY PROFILE

If your total points score was . . .

40–50: You know that you were created by God on purpose. You know that you have a purpose in life. You are secure in your identity. You have a good support system of family and friends. You may enjoy hobbies and activities, but you are not defined by what you do or what you are good at. You are aware that if Jesus Christ is your Savior, your eternity is secure in Him.

30–39: You might see yourself as a human *doing*. Instead, try to see yourself as a human *being*. If we identify ourselves by what we do, our identity is shaken. It can crumble if we perform poorly.

20–29: It's never too late to understand that you can have an identity that is secure in Jesus Christ. He is a Rock, who loves you unconditionally, who never changes, and who will never forsake you or leave you alone. God has given each of us gifts and made each of us uniquely and wonderfully. By spending time learning His Word, we can learn what our gifts are and the purpose He has for our lives. Go through this key again with your Guide, and pray that you understand that God made you to follow His purpose for your life.

KINGDOM KEY 2
INTEGRITY

GOALS

1. You will discover what integrity is.
2. You will see how you rate yourself on integrity.
3. You will read about what can happen if you don't have integrity.

MEANING

Seeking to live honestly and right; complete and steadfast

INTEGRITY

- **HONEST**—free from deception; speaking and living the truth
- **DECENT**—well-formed; marked by a right heart and actions
- **COMPLETE**—not limited or lacking in any necessary area

Application: You have a commitment to biblical truth and honesty. You have good character that is consistent and dependable. You choose thoughts, words, and actions that reflect what is right and honest.

FROM THE WORD

People who don't believe might say you are doing wrong. But lead good lives among them. Then they will see your good deeds. And they will give glory to God on the day he comes to judge. **—1 Peter 2:12**

DEFINE

What does "integrity" mean to you?

~~to be Honst~~

Integrity means to be Honest.

Intagrity means to not Do bad things

It means to trust GOD.

QUESTIONS 2 PONDER

1. Do your friends make it easier or more difficult for you to do what is right? Do your friends listen to you if you ask them to do what is right?
2. Has another person's poor choices (lack of integrity) made life more difficult for you? (For example, has someone ever stolen something from you? Bullied you? How did that affect you?)
3. How do you want others to describe you: [Your name] is a person who is good, responsive, and fun.

JUST 4 FUN

Get a bag of knotted or circle pretzels, the ones with the holes in them. (You can also use O-shaped cereal pieces.) Stack them as high as you can in a tower. Then, blow on the tower. It falls easily, doesn't it! Now stack the pretzels again, but this time use a base made from a stick of butter or margarine—a three-tablespoon block should do the trick. Stack the pretzels again, but this time stick five or six pieces of dried spaghetti running up and down the stack like a spine. Make sure the spaghetti is pushed into the butter. Blow on it. The pretzel tower is sturdier when it has the butter base and spaghetti pieces to keep it up.

Another word for a tower or a building is *structure*. *Structural integrity* is a builder's word to describe what keeps a building standing. It describes the internal strength of a high-rise, house, or tower. The pretzel tower with the spaghetti had structural integrity. The tower without spaghetti fell because it lacked integrity.

Personal integrity keeps your character strong. It's like having extra strength—some spaghetti!—in your life. Personal integrity describes your thoughts, words, and actions that combine to make your life steady. It describes the internal strength of a person.

Just as a stack of pretzels alone falls easily, a life without personal integrity can topple in a moment. It's important to build your life in a way that prevents it from falling.

HERE 2 HELP

Maintaining your personal integrity is important. You don't want your reputation to collapse. It can come crumbling down in a moment with one wrong decision. For example, one bad choice to cheat on an exam can put a stain on your school career. One lie can collapse a friendship. One stolen video game can get you in trouble with the police.

For you to advance through the different levels of life, your integrity must be intact. Your legs need to be strong with honesty, your arms powerful with right choices (decency). Your body, mind, and spirit should be strong. You should act with a pure heart and consistency. You should be seeking to do what is right.

HERE 2 HELP (CONTINUED)

One system to make decisions that result in strong choices is called **STAR**. The **STAR** principle tells you to

 Stop what you are doing;

 Think about how your decisions will impact yourself and others;

 Adjust your decisions; and

 Respond thoughtfully.

Over the next few days, memorize the **STAR** principle and use it to make choices.

IT'S UP 2 YOU

Read each statement. Then select the response that best describes your reaction to the following statements. Follow the directions on tallying your score at the end of the quiz. Ask your Guide for help if you have questions.

1. If I had a chance to steal something from a store, I would do it.
   A. DEFINITELY B. MAYBE C. NO, I WOULDN'T DO THAT.

2. If I want to do something but my mom or dad disapproves of it, I would do it anyway.
   A. DEFINITELY B. MAYBE C. NO, I DON'T DO THAT.

3. I go to websites and download videos and/or music without paying. I don't find out if it's legal or not.
   A. DEFINITELY B. MAYBE C. NO, I DON'T DO THAT.

4. It is perfectly okay to copy homework as long as the other person doesn't mind.
   A. DEFINITELY B. MAYBE C. NO, I DON'T DO THAT.

5. I think about how my decisions and actions affect my family and/or friends.
   A. DEFINITELY B. MAYBE C. NO, I DON'T DO THAT.

6. I think about how my decisions and actions affect people I don't know.
   A. DEFINITELY B. MAYBE C. NO, I DON'T DO THAT

7. If I thought a kid at school was cheating on a test, I would tell a teacher.
   A. DEFINITELY
   B. MAYBE
   C. NO, I WOULDN'T SNITCH.
   D. I'D TALK ABOUT IT WITH A PARENT OR MENTOR BEFORE TELLING THE TEACHER.

8. Everyone who knows me would say they can count on me to be truthful.
   A. ALL OF THE TIME
   B. MOST OF THE TIME
   C. SOMETIMES
   D. NEVER

9. I say and do things so that other people will like me.
   A. ALL OF THE TIME
   B. MOST OF THE TIME
   C. SOMETIMES
   D. NEVER

LET INTEGRITY AND UPRIGHTNESS PRESERVE ME, FOR I WAIT FOR YOU.

PSALM 25:21, NASB

IT'S UP 2 YOU (CONTINUED)

INTEGRITY SCORECARD

For each question, assign the following point values for the answer chosen. Then, total the number of points you have on the assessment.

1. Answer:	A-2	B-4	C-6		POINTS:	6
2. Answer:	A-2	B-4	C-6		POINTS:	4
3. Answer:	A-2	B-4	C-6		POINTS:	6
4. Answer:	A-2	B-4	C-6		POINTS:	6
5. Answer:	A-6	B-4	C-2		POINTS:	4
6. Answer:	A-6	B-4	C-2		POINTS:	2
7. Answer:	A-6	B-4	C-2	D-6	POINTS:	6
8. Answer:	A-8	B-6	C-4	D-2	POINTS:	6
9. Answer:	A-2	B-4	C-6	D-8	POINTS:	6

TOTAL POINTS: 46

INTEGRITY PROFILE

If your total points score was . . .

46–58: You are walking with integrity. You are doing the right thing even when the right thing is difficult to do or might be unpopular. You are putting the welfare of others ahead of your own needs or wants. You are asking for guidance from the right places.

32–44: If you answered in this range, take a moment to thank the people in your life who have taught you that it is important to do the right thing. But from time to time you struggle to do what you know is right. Understand that doing what you know to be right and true will become a habit if you are consistent.

18–30: Sometimes kids (and adults!) have to be awakened to the idea that the community is full of people—some of whom we may never meet—who count on us to do the right thing. Every time you get in a car to go somewhere, you are counting on everyone else to obey the traffic laws so that you can safely arrive at your destination. If your score is in this range, get into the habit of using the **STAR** principle (see the Here 2 Help section) as you make decisions. Ask your Guide to go through this key with you again.

KINGDOM KEY 3
WISDOM

GOALS

1. You will distinguish between God's wisdom and what the world says.
2. You will explore negative consequences of bad choices.
3. You will understand where to find wisdom and how to get it.

MEANING

Good sense of judgment—the ability to apply understanding to life's choices

- **REASONABLE**—having sound judgment and good thinking; making sense
- **DISCERNMENT**—being able to grasp and comprehend what is difficult to understand or see
- **APPLY**—to put to use, especially for some practical purpose

Application: You have the ability to make positive and productive decisions; you can communicate with others in a reasonable way.

FROM THE WORD

Real wisdom, God's wisdom, begins with a holy life and is characterized by getting along with others. It is gentle and reasonable, overflowing with mercy and blessings, not hot one day and cold the next, not two-faced.
—James 3:17, MSG

DEFINE

What does "wisdom" mean to you?

QUESTIONS 2 PONDER

1. What is the difference between being smart and being wise?
2. What are things you can do to grow in understanding God's wise ways?
3. Can you name one person you consider to be wise and explain why you chose him or her?

JUST 4 FUN

1. Write down daily-life scenarios on index cards or small sheets of paper. These scenarios can be real or could-be-real situations. They can involve friends, family, or strangers. One example: A friend of a friend brought a smartphone to a church overnight event. He/she is planning on showing everyone inappropriate images. Your friend tells you about it, but he or she asks you not to tell. What should you do? Another example: Your friend's older brother offers you a ride on his new motorcycle. You're tempted to take the ride because it looks like so much fun, but your parents aren't available to give permission. What should you do?
2. One at a time, select one of these life scenarios and think about how you might handle it. Discuss with your Guide or fellow soldiers how to wisely deal with each scenario.

HERE 2 HELP

Life is full of decisions, and you have made some wrong ones—just like everyone else. Pretend you were given the chance to redo moments in your life. What would you do differently? Would you make better choices? Would you choose different friends? How would you spend your time? Would you practice harder at whatever sport, gift, or skill you have? Do your homework on time? Give up electronic games and TV programs for a year? (Okay, maybe that last one is a stretch!) If you answered yes to any of those questions, then you know what it means to apply wisdom to life's situations. By answering yes, it shows you want to go back and make a different choice, this time with the wisdom of hindsight.

Wisdom is the ability to understand the best way to approach something and act on it. However, wisdom won't help if you don't apply that understanding.

Life is not like a video game. We don't get zapped or destroyed when we make unwise choices (thankfully). However, our bad choices set us back in other ways. They could

- wound a friendship;
- damage your lungs or health;
- ruin your reputation;
- block your chances to move to a higher-level sports team;
- get you into trouble at school;
- involve you in a car accident; or
- disappoint your parents or other mentors.

Whatever it is, unwise choices stop you from moving forward.

On the other hand, wisdom is a powerful key to unlocking doors to

- a better future;
- more enjoyable friendships;
- a greater position on the team or choir or orchestra;
- buying your own cell phone;
- opportunities in school;
- peace of mind when it comes to your physical body; and
- greater access to the power of prayer.

Wisdom moves you forward. Use this key to open doors, jump higher, run faster, defeat the enemy's schemes, and more!

IF ANY OF YOU LACKS WISDOM, LET HIM ASK OF GOD, WHO GIVES TO ALL GENEROUSLY AND WITHOUT REPROACH, AND IT WILL BE GIVEN TO HIM.

JAMES 1:5, NASB

IT'S UP 2 YOU

Read each statement. Then select the response that best represents how you think and feel. Circle the answer that corresponds to that response. Then follow the instructions to fill in your Wisdom Meter on page 22. Ask your Guide for help if you have questions.

1. When I'm not sure what to do, I ask a parent or mentor what the Bible says to do. Or I read the Bible myself.
   A. YES B. NO C. SOMETIMES

2. When I'm not sure which decision is best, I pray about what to do.
   A. YES B. NO C. SOMETIMES

3. I tend to repeat the same mistakes.
   A. YES B. NO C. SOMETIMES

4. When I'm faced with a tough decision, I ask people who have experience what to do.
   A. YES B. NO C. SOMETIMES

5. The elderly don't understand what my life is like.
   A. TRUE B. FALSE C. MAYBE

6. I have at least one adult in my life whom I can trust to give me good advice.
   A. YES B. NO

7. Church friends my age are a good source of advice. I talk to them before I make decisions.
   A. YES B. NO C. SOMETIMES

8. When others ask me for advice, I give them my opinion confidently.
   A. YES, THAT'S ME!
   B. I'M OFTEN HESITANT TO ANSWER. I'M NOT SURE WHAT I BELIEVE. I SUGGEST THAT THEY SHOULD ASK AN ADULT.
   C. SOMETIMES, BUT THERE ARE TIMES WHEN I'M A LITTLE AFRAID TO TELL PEOPLE WHAT I THINK.

9. I wait until I feel sure of something before I act or speak.
   A. YES B. NO C. SOMETIMES

10. I can remember a time when I followed advice that I didn't like, but I knew it was right.
    A. YES; IT WORKED WELL FOR ME.
    B. NO, BUT I WISH I HAD AND WILL NEXT TIME.
    C. NO, I HAVEN'T HAD THAT EXPERIENCE.

WISDOM SCORECARD

Record your answers here.

1. Answer:	A-2	B-0	C-1	POINTS:
2. Answer:	A-2	B-0	C-1	POINTS:
3. Answer:	A-0	B-2	C-1	POINTS:
4. Answer:	A-2	B-0	C-1	POINTS:
5. Answer:	A-0	B-2	C-1	POINTS:
6. Answer:	A-1	B-0		POINTS:
7. Answer:	A-2	B-0	C-1	POINTS:
8. Answer:	A-2	B-0	C-1	POINTS:
9. Answer:	A-2	B-0	C-1	POINTS:
10. Answer:	A-2	B-1	C-0	POINTS:

TOTAL POINTS: ☐

IT'S UP 2 YOU (CONTINUED)

WISDOM METER

Color in the Wisdom Meter according to your scorecard. If your total points score was . . .

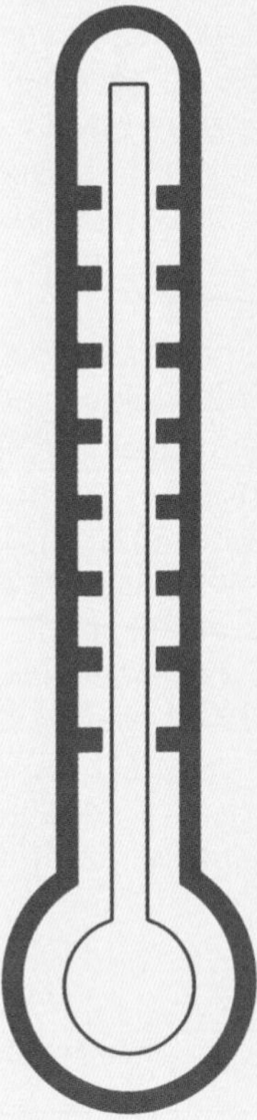

14–19 points: You've already learned that wisdom can be found through others who have more life experience. You have also applied biblical truth to life experiences. Wisdom is a lifelong pursuit, so keep up the good work.

8–13 points: You're on your way to walking in wisdom. The Bible teaches that respect and awe of the Lord are the beginning of knowledge. Continue seeking His will and learning about His character through Bible study and prayer. Wisdom will save you from many painful experiences in life. When offering advice to others, seek God's wisdom about what to say.

0–7 points: The Bible tells us that if we ask God for wisdom, He will give it to us (James 1:5–6). If you find that you're not learning from experience and are often making unwise choices, be sure to find a reliable adult you can seek out for advice. More important, read God's Word daily. (Hint: Proverbs is a book that is full of practical wisdom.) Also, take time to talk with/listen to God about what you know and what you need to learn. He is listening and desires to teach you.

LEVEL II
MY POWER

MEANING

Communication with and/or making a request of God

PRAYER

- **ABIDE**—be around someone enough to know them well
- **ASK**—to make a request of
- **ACCESS**—having permission or the right to make use of something

Application: Prayer is a kingdom kid's primary weapon of warfare. With it, you can touch heaven and change earth. The secret to prayer is not praying for a long time or using fancy words. The secret is in discovering God's will and then asking for it. To put prayer last is to put God last. To put prayer first is to put God first.

FROM THE WORD

The prayer of a godly person is powerful. Things happen because of it. Elijah was a human being, just as we are. He prayed hard that it wouldn't rain. And it didn't rain on the land for three and a half years. **—James 5:16-17**

DEFINE

What does "prayer" mean to you?

QUESTIONS 2 PONDER

1. What are some things that stop you from praying?
2. Can you describe a time that you prayed for something and God answered you?
3. Do you think that God always answers our prayers? Why or why not?

JUST 4 FUN

Make a prayer jar. (You could also use a journal.) Find an empty jar or plastic container and decorate it. At the beginning of each day, write a short prayer on a slip of paper about the size of a Chinese-cookie fortune. The prayer can be whatever you want to tell God, or it can be a request you have. Offer up this prayer to God, and then place the paper in your jar. At the end of the week, reread the prayer requests. See how the Lord has heard your prayers and responded.

HERE 2 HELP

Sometimes car dealerships mail out car keys and letters to thousands of people. The letter asks you to come to the car dealership and put your key in the ignition of a brand-new car. If the car starts, you win it! If the car doesn't start, you get nothing. You might as well throw the key away.

Prayer is like a key. When it's the right key in the right car, amazing things can happen. However, many people don't know how to use this key. They feel as if prayer doesn't work for them, so they throw it away. Maybe it's as if they tried using their key to start the wrong car or open a locker at school. Since nothing happened, they assumed the key wasn't worth much anyhow.

God has given us the secret to the power of prayer. He tells us that the secret to getting this prayer key to work is Jesus Christ. He is the ignition. Listen to what Jesus says: "If you make yourselves at home with me and my words are at home in you, you can be sure that whatever you ask will be listened to and acted upon" (John 15:7, MSG).

In case you didn't understand what He meant in that verse, read this one: "From now on, whatever you request along the lines of who I am and what I am doing, I'll do it. That's how the Father will be seen for who he is in the Son. I mean it. Whatever you request in this way, I'll do" (John 14:13–14, MSG).

He means it. Whatever you ask for—when it matches with His character and biblical truth, and will bring the most glory to His name—He'll do it. The secret to the prayer key is not in the number of minutes you spend praying. It's not whether you pray with your eyes open or shut. The secret to prayer is in hanging out (abiding) with Jesus. That means allowing His Word to remain in your heart. That way you'll be asking for things He wants you to do, have, be, and become.

If you place this kingdom key in the ignition (power) of Jesus Christ and follow what He's doing, where He's going, and what He wants you to do . . . then you win. He will open the door (Matthew 7:7).

IT'S UP 2 YOU

Pray using Bible verses as a guide. Select Bible verses to turn into prayers. This is called *praying Scripture.* Here's one example from Matthew 25:45:

> He will answer them, "I'm telling the solemn truth: Whenever you failed to do one of these things to someone who was being overlooked or ignored, that was me—you failed to do it to me." (MSG)

Turn this verse into a prayer like this: *God, help me to reach out to those being overlooked or ignored in my world and to treat them as Your loved children.* Or select a psalm as an inspiration for prayer and write it as a prayer. Do Psalm 63:3–4 for practice.

Your love is better than life.

____

____

So I will bring glory to you with my lips.

____

____

I will praise you as long as I live.

____

____

I will call on your name when I lift up my hands in prayer.

____

____

IT'S UP 2 YOU (CONTINUED)

Give thanks. Get a single sheet of paper or a prayer journal. Gather colored pens or pencils. List things in your life or in the world for which you are thankful. Write all over the page—create a word cloud—and if you are feeling artistic, doodle images of the things you are thankful for today.

Wait. Pretend you have just pulled into the drive-through lane at a fast-food restaurant. Next, you give the cashier your order. Do you keep telling the cashier over and over what you ordered while you wait? No, when you order your food, you wait for it to come. This is because you trust and expect it to come.

The secret to living a life with the power of prayer is in knowing what to ask. Jesus says that if you ask anything that is in line with God's will, He will do it. Anything! List some things that you know are in line with God's will. Here are two powerful requests to start with: asking God to give you wisdom and asking God to reveal His purposes to you for your life.

THE PRAYERS OF HONEST PEOPLE PLEASE [GOD].

PROVERBS 15:8

KINGDOM KEY 5
GOD'S WORD

GOALS

1. You will learn formulas (using the acronyms REAP and SPECK) for understanding God's Word.
2. You will practice reading God's Word.
3. You will learn how to study key Scriptures.

MEANING

Sacred writings found in the Old and New Testament, the books of the Bible

GOD'S WORD

- **INSPIRED**—having a divine cause or influence
- **TRUTH**—commitment to an original or to a standard; the real facts about something
- **POWERFUL**—having a strong effect on someone or something

Application: The Word of God is one of the weapons of warfare. It is the sword of the Spirit. Its ability to defeat Satan with truth is similar to how light overtakes darkness. It also guides, directs, and reveals areas where we need to grow.

FROM THE WORD

There's nothing like the written Word of God for showing you the way to salvation through faith in Christ Jesus. Every part of Scripture is God-breathed and useful one way or another—showing us truth, exposing our rebellion, correcting our mistakes, training us to live God's way. Through the Word we are put together and shaped up for the tasks God has for us.
—2 Timothy 3:16-17, MSG

DEFINE

What does "God's Word" mean to you?

QUESTIONS 2 PONDER

1. Do you have more pop songs memorized or Bible verses?
2. What is one verse that has made a difference in your life? Explain how.
3. What stops you from studying the Bible more? What do you need to do to find time to read the Bible today? Tomorrow? Next week?

JUST 4 FUN

Play the Land-Mine Game with your Guide. This game demonstrates the importance of listening to God's voice.

1. Allow your Guide to blindfold you and lead you through the "minefield." The minefield represents daily life and the obstacles Satan tries to place in our way. The minefield can consist of puddles of water, obstacles, barriers, things to step over, etc.
2. As you walk through the minefield, your Guide will instruct you on how to maneuver around or through the obstacles. It's important for you to listen carefully to your Guide so that you don't get tripped up by the obstacles. This demonstrates how important it is to know God's voice so we can avoid setbacks in our world.

[JESUS SAID,] "BLESSED ARE THOSE WHO HEAR GOD'S WORD AND OBEY IT."

LUKE 11:28

HERE 2 HELP

The Bible is a big book that teaches us important stuff for life. How can we learn it?

The answer to that question is in another question: How do you eat an elephant?

One bite at a time.

I'm not expecting you to digest the whole Bible after school one afternoon. Instead, take the Bible bit by bit—or bite by bite—as you learn and study God's truth and principles.

If you want to go deeper in your understanding of this powerful kingdom key—God's Word—here's a tip called **REAP**. It's a memory device to help you understand and use God's Word. Here's how it works:

R—Read a passage or verse.

E—Examine the passage or verse. What phrases or bits of information stick out? What questions do you have? What can you learn through this passage?

A—Apply His Word to your life. How can you practice what you have learned? Set a goal so you can measure what you have learned.

P—Pray and ask God for opportunities to apply what you learned. Also ask for His help to use the knowledge and understanding you gained.

IT'S UP 2 YOU

Use the verses in this Kingdom Quest strategy guide or select your own verses to study. As you read the verse, use the ***SPECK*** *method to see how it applies to you. Answer any or all the questions below from the verse. Start by examining one verse of your choice and write your answers on the following lines. Start a* ***SPECK*** *journal or enter your notes on an electronic device.*

S—Is there a **sin** for me to avoid?

P—Is there a **promise** for me to claim?

E—Is there an **example** for me to follow?

C—Is there a **commandment** for me to obey?

K—Is there **knowledge** I can gain?

VERSE

S

P

E

C

K

KINGDOM KEY 6

FAITH

GOALS

1. You will do an object lesson to teach you about having strong faith.
2. You will learn how to apply faith through a life example.
3. You will fill out your own faith scorecard.

MEANING

Strong belief or trust in someone or something; belief in the existence of God; strong religious feelings or beliefs

FAITH

- **BELIEF**—a state of mind or habit in which trust or confidence is placed in some person or thing
- **CREDENCE**—belief that something is true
- **TRUST**—belief that someone or something is reliable, good, or honest

Application: Faith is acting as if God is telling the truth. Faith involves more than your feelings; it involves your feet. We are to walk by faith, not only talk by faith.

FROM THE WORD

[Jesus said,] "Suppose you have faith as small as a mustard seed. Then you can say to this mulberry tree, 'Be pulled up. Be planted in the sea.' And it will obey you." **—Luke 17:6**

DEFINE

What does "faith" mean to you?

____

____

____

____

____

QUESTIONS 2 PONDER

1. Can you describe a time when you doubted God or His Word? What did you do to rebuild your faith?
2. Besides God, name three things you know to be true even though you have never seen them.
3. Finish this: Sometimes I don't believe ____________________.

JUST 4 FUN

Faith is invisible, but it's strong. Hebrews 11:1 says, "Faith is being sure of what we hope for. It is being sure of what we do not see."

For a simple object lesson to demonstrate this spiritual principle, gather two empty, clean two-liter soda bottles, one bottle cap, and a broom. Put the lid on one of the empty bottles. Leave the other one uncapped. Clear a large area on the floor. Lay the bottles on the floor lengthwise. Next, take the broom's handle and whack the bottles using *medium force*. As you'll see, the bottle without the lid (without faith) crushes. The bottle with the lid (the one full of faith) resists the blow.

This is like invisible faith. Faith can be tested when trials come. Like the bottle with the lid, we can resist the blows of doubt.

HERE 2 HELP

A few years ago, an interesting event occurred at a crusade held at a stadium in South Carolina. More than 25,000 people had gathered in the stadium when storm clouds formed. The leaders of the crusade and I (one of the speakers) went into a small room to pray that the rain wouldn't affect the crusade.

In the midst of our prayers, a petite woman named Linda came forward. She boldly prayed, "I ask in the name of the Lord Jesus Christ for the rain to stop for the sake of Your name!"

With that, we opened our eyes. Eyebrows went up. All we could think was *Whoa. Did she really just pray that?* We went back outside to the stage.

At 7:00 p.m., the sky became entirely black. The music started and massive thunder and lightning surrounded us. People stirred in their seats. While umbrellas began to go up, Linda sat in her seat with a confident look on her face.

Then a wall of water rushed toward the stadium. Yet when the rain hit the stadium, it split. The two sides of rain met around the stadium.

The preachers and leaders looked at each other. Then we looked at Linda, who stared straight ahead confidently.

I believe God paid special attention to Linda's prayer because she had great faith.*

Type in this URL or scan the QR code to watch a video on this powerful prayer story you read about in today's Here2Help: https://www.youtube.com/watch?v=zE7YomvT2eo&list=UURZweRCzcK5ObXPCNKvdMO.

*Adapted with permission from Tony Evans and Chrystal Evans Hurst, *Kingdom Woman: Embracing Your Purpose, Power, and Possibilities* (Carol Stream, IL: Tyndale House Publishers, 2013), 73–75.

IT'S IMPOSSIBLE TO PLEASE GOD APART FROM FAITH. AND WHY? BECAUSE ANYONE WHO WANTS TO APPROACH GOD MUST BELIEVE BOTH THAT HE EXISTS *AND* THAT HE CARES ENOUGH TO RESPOND TO THOSE WHO SEEK HIM.

HEBREWS 11:6, MSG

IT'S UP 2 YOU

Read each statement. Then select the answer that best reflects the way you would respond to challenging situations. Circle the letter that corresponds with that answer. Follow the directions on tallying your score at the end of the quiz. Ask your Guide for help if you have questions.

1. I believe that God's Word is always true, all the time.
   A. STRONGLY AGREE B. AGREE C. DISAGREE D. STRONGLY DISAGREE

2. I tend to get discouraged when I'm waiting on God to answer a prayer.
   A. STRONGLY AGREE B. AGREE C. DISAGREE D. STRONGLY DISAGREE

3. I have made a decision or acted on faith and it turned out well.
   A. YES, MANY TIMES
   B. OCCASIONALLY
   C. MAYBE ONCE
   D. NO, NOT THAT I KNOW OF.

4. I have made a decision or acted on faith and it turned out to be a disappointment.
   A. YES, MANY TIMES
   B. OCCASIONALLY
   C. MAYBE ONCE
   D. NO, I HAVE NEVER BEEN DISAPPOINTED.

5. Fear holds me back from trying new things.
   A. STRONGLY AGREE B. AGREE C. DISAGREE D. STRONGLY DISAGREE

6. I need to see it before I can believe it.
   A. ALWAYS
   B. MOST OF THE TIME
   C. SOMETIMES
   D. NO. IF I CAN IMAGINE IT, I CAN BELIEVE IT.

7. I make decisions based on how I feel about the situation or the people involved.
   A. STRONGLY AGREE B. AGREE C. DISAGREE D. STRONGLY DISAGREE

8. I regularly pray for God's help and guidance.
   A. YES, AT LEAST ONCE A DAY
   B. YES, OFTEN
   C. YES, EVERY SUNDAY AT CHURCH
   D. YES, WHEN I'M WORRIED OR IN A BIND

9. I believe that God always answers prayer.
   A. STRONGLY AGREE   B. AGREE   C. DISAGREE   D. STRONGLY DISAGREE

10. Sometimes, things get worse before they get better.
   A. STRONGLY AGREE   B. AGREE   C. DISAGREE   D. STRONGLY DISAGREE

FAITH SCORECARD

1. Answer:	A-5	B-4	C-3	D-2	POINTS:
2. Answer:	A-2	B-3	C-4	D-5	POINTS:
3. Answer:	A-5	B-4	C-3	D-2	POINTS:
4. Answer:	A-2	B-3	C-4	D-5	POINTS:
5. Answer:	A-2	B-3	C-4	D-5	POINTS:
6. Answer:	A-2	B-3	C-4	D-5	POINTS:
7. Answer:	A-5	B-4	C-3	D-2	POINTS:
8. Answer:	A-5	B-4	C-3	D-2	POINTS:
9. Answer:	A-5	B-4	C-3	D-2	POINTS:
10. Answer:	A-2	B-3	C-4	D-5	POINTS:

TOTAL POINTS: ☐

IT'S UP 2 YOU (CONTINUED)

FAITH PROFILE

If your total points score was . . .

40–50: You have learned the excitement of living by faith. God always answers prayer, but He doesn't always answer on our timetable or always give us the answer we want. The longer we walk with God, the more we learn that He always has our best interests in mind. We also learn that He is always true to His Word.

30–39: Building your faith, like anything else worth doing, requires practice. That practice comes through prayer, worship, and studying God's Word. When we believe His Word to be true for all people and at all times, it changes the way we view life. We begin to see that sometimes what we wanted really isn't the best for us. We learn to trust that God will provide for all our needs "according to His riches in glory in Christ Jesus" (Philippians 4:19, NASB).

20–29: One thing is for sure: "There is now no condemnation for those who are in Christ Jesus" (Romans 8:1, NASB). God wants you to have faith because through faith, He can bless you, guide you, and otherwise make your life full. Never let anyone tell you that life with God is dull. Nothing can be further from the truth! Living by faith is the most exciting way to live. God wants to bless you abundantly, above what you can dream or imagine (Ephesians 3:20). Start talking to God today. He is listening. Read His Word, and sing Him a love song. He is waiting!

LEVEL III
MY SKILLS

KINGDOM KEY 7

RESPONSIBILITY

GOALS

1. You will learn about the rewards of being a responsible person.
2. You will learn how to prepare a budget.
3. You will discover different areas in which you are to be responsible.

MEANING

Able to be trusted to do what is right or to do the things that are expected or required

- **GIVE**—to transfer from oneself to another, either through time, talents, objects, or money
- **RECONCILE**—to restore a friendship, to make amends and reunite
- **TRUSTED**—reality that someone or something is reliable, good, honest, and dependable

Application: Responsibility means being trustworthy in any given situation: your money, how you treat others, your time, your schoolwork, and any number of things. It could be as simple as rinsing off your dishes. It could be as complex as being a good sport and a good friend.

FROM THE WORD

Whoever is generous to the poor lends to the LORD, and he will repay him for his deed. **—Proverbs 19:17, ESV**

DEFINE

What does "responsibility" mean to you?

____

____

____

____

____

QUESTIONS 2 PONDER

1. What are some of the benefits of being responsible at home? In friendships? At school?
2. What is one area where you can grow in responsibility? What steps can you take?
3. Does being responsible scare you? Why or why not?
4. Are you responsible for anyone other than yourself?

JUST 4 FUN

Read the following story and discuss the questions at the end.

THE LITTLE RED HEN

A little red hen lived in a barnyard. She spent almost all of her time walking about the barnyard, scratching everywhere for worms. She had a lot of chicks to feed.

One day the little red hen found a seed. The horse, who pulled the farmer's plow and had seen the seeds before, told her it was a wheat seed. The horse said the seed would sprout and grow. And when it was ripe, it could be milled into flour and then made into bread. Then the farmer came and took the horse to the fields.

Now the little red hen knew the seed ought to be planted. She called loudly to her friends: "Who will help me plant the seed?"

The pig said, "Not I."

And the cat said, "Not I."

And the rat said, "Not I."

"Well, then," said the little red hen, "I will." And she did.

Then she went on with her daily duties through the long summer days, scratching for worms and feeding her chicks. Meanwhile the pig grew fat, and the cat grew fat, and the rat grew fat. But the wheat grew tall and ready for harvest.

One day the little red hen noticed how large the wheat was and that the grain was ripe. She asked her friends: "Who will help me cut the wheat?"

The pig said, "Not I."

And the cat said, "Not I."

And the rat said, "Not I."

"Well, then," said the little red hen, "I will." And she did.

She got the sickle from among the farmer's tools in the barn and proceeded to cut down the big plant of wheat. On the ground lay the nicely cut wheat, ready to be gathered and threshed.

Again, in a very hopeful tone, she called out, "Who will help me thresh the wheat and carry it to the mill?"

The pig said, "Not I."

And the cat said, "Not I."

And the rat said, "Not I."

So the good little red hen could do nothing but say, "I will then." And she did. Carrying the sack of wheat, she trudged off to the distant mill. There she ordered the wheat ground into beautiful white flour. After the miller brought her the flour, she walked slowly back all the way to her own barnyard.

After all this hard work, the little red hen was tired, and she went to sleep early. She would have liked to sleep late in the morning, but her chicks woke her up early with their peeping. She got up, fluffed her feathers, and thought, *Today I need to make the bread.*

So she hunted up the pig, the cat, and the rat. She asked them, "Who will help me make the bread?"

Alas for the little red hen! Once more her hopes were dashed!

The pig said, "Not I."

And the cat said, "Not I."

And the rat said, "Not I."

So the little red hen said once more, "I will then." And she did.

First of all she set the dough, as was proper. When it was time she kneaded the dough, divided it into loaves, and put them into the oven to bake.

All the while the cat, the rat, and the pig sat lazily by, giggling and chuckling.

At last the great moment arrived. A delicious smell filled the barn. The little red hen took the loaves out of the oven.

Then she called, "Who will help me eat the bread?"

The pig said, "I will."

And the cat said, "I will."

And the rat said, "I will."

But the little red hen said, "No, you won't. My chicks and I will." And the little red hen and her baby chicks ate all the delicious bread.*

*Adapted from *The Little Red Hen*, an English folktale retold by Florence White Williams (Chicago: Saalfield Publishing, 1918).

JUST 4 FUN (CONTINUED)

1. Are you more like the little red hen, her chicks, or the three lazy friends? Explain your answer.
2. The little red hen had to act alone. She could have given up, thinking, *Well, if no one's going to help me, I'll just quit. I can't do it on my own.* Why do you think she kept going?
3. Is there a task in your life that seems overwhelming? How can breaking it into steps help you accomplish your task?
4. Pick one of the following community jobs and tell what would happen if every worker in the city woke up one morning and said, "I'm not going to do my job today": police officer, doctor, truck driver, school teacher.

HONOR GOD WITH EVERYTHING YOU OWN; GIVE HIM THE FIRST AND THE BEST.

PROVERBS 3:9, MSG

HERE 2 HELP

A long time ago, four Israelite teens were captured and taken to serve in the king's court. Here's part of their story:

> The king told [his chief advisor] to bring him some of the Israelites. The king wanted them to serve him in his court. He wanted nobles and men from the royal family. He was looking for young men who were healthy and handsome. They had to be able to learn anything. They had to be well educated. They had to have the ability to understand new things quickly and easily. The king wanted men who could serve in his palace. [The chief advisor] was supposed to teach them the Babylonian language and writings. (Daniel 1:3–4)

The four Israelite teens, Daniel and his friends, were then enrolled in a three-year college of sorts—a king's college. The king's goal was to change the teens. He wanted to get the teens to forget Israelite culture and religion and instead learn the king's culture and religion. The teens took classes and completed assignments. They were responsible in every way.

But when they were told to eat certain types of meat, they asked to be excused. Eating such food went against what Daniel and his friends had been taught. This meat wasn't clean for their spirits or their bodies. They asked to be given vegetables instead. They stood against the king's orders and asked for special consideration.

Daniel and his friends remained responsible in this area—keeping their values in place. The king and his council discovered that Daniel and his friends' "appearance seemed better" (Daniel 1:15, NASB) and so they were allowed to continue the special diet. Over time, they advanced in leadership. In fact, Daniel eventually rose to a position of great influence in the new land.

Responsibility means more than putting your dishes away after you're finished eating, although that's a good thing to do. It means more than completing and submitting your homework, which is also a good thing to do. Responsibility means living up to your standards and values. Not only this, but you're to also look out for other people as well as yourself.

When you act responsibly day after day, your hard work may be your only reward. Not many people will notice. However, being responsible will enable you to reach your goals, gain the respect of others, and make a difference anywhere and everywhere.

IT'S UP 2 YOU

Find four jars, envelopes, small boxes, or any easy-to-store containers that will hold coins and paper money. Decorate the containers and label them GIVING, LONG-TERM SAVINGS, SHORT-TERM SAVINGS, and SPENDING.

With your guide, determine what portion of your money should go into each category. One common standard is putting 10 percent into each of the giving and long-term savings containers. (It is easy to calculate 10 percent. You just move the decimal point one place to the left. For example, if you have $9.86, then 10 percent would be $0.98 or 98 cents.) The other 80 percent is for you to spend on short-term savings items or activities, gifts for others, and personal use.

First, determine who will be the recipient of your giving money. Some should be given to your church on a weekly or monthly basis. You could also set aside some of the giving funds as a special gift to a missionary or as a donation to the local soup kitchen. (Your Guide can help you find ways to do that.)

Second, set at least one long-term savings goal. This purchase should take you about a year to save for: A new bike? A cell phone? A pair of earrings for your mom?

Third, set some short-term savings goals. Is your brother having a birthday soon? Is there a movie you really want to see in the theater? Do you need a backpack?

Fourth, do the math. (You may need a calculator and help from your Guide!) How much money will you need to earn per week to meet your goals? Determine with your Guide whether you'll need to do additional chores at home to earn money. If earning extra cash at home isn't an option, your Guide can help you brainstorm ways to earn money outside the home. Use the following sample budget to help you determine your income needs.

SAVINGS AND SPENDING PLAN

INCOME

Allowance/chore income per week:______________

Outside-the-home income per week: ____________

Miscellaneous gift/award
income per year: ______________, divided by 52 = _______________

WEEKLY INCOME ESTIMATE: ☐ **TOTAL A**

GIVING AND SPENDING

Giving to church per month: _________, divided by 4 = _________

Giving to others per month: __________, divided by 4 = _________

Personal spending money per week: __________

WEEKLY GIVING/SPENDING ESTIMATE: ☐ **TOTAL B**

SAVINGS

Long-term savings goal for one year: ______, divided by 52 = ______

Short-term savings for goal no. 1 ______ (divide by the number of weeks you have to save for it) = ______

Short-term savings goal no. 2 ______ (divide by the number of weeks you have to save for it) = ______

WEEKLY SAVINGS ESTIMATE: ☐ **TOTAL C**

DO THE MATH

Add Total B ________ + Total C _________ = (Total D) _________.

Which is larger? Total A or Total D?

If Total A is larger, congratulations! You have enough income to meet your needs.

If Total D is larger than Total A, then you need to make a plan to either earn more money to make up the difference, or you need to cut back your spending. Your Guide can help you plan for your income needs.

LOVE ONE ANOTHER DEEPLY. HONOR OTHERS MORE THAN YOURSELVES. STAY EXCITED ABOUT YOUR FAITH AS YOU SERVE THE LORD.

ROMANS 12:10-11

KINGDOM KEY 8

SERVICE

GOALS

1. You will discover different levels of service.
2. You will find ways to serve others.
3. You will be able to define what service means to you.

MEANING

A useful act meant to help another person or a group of people

SERVICE

- **ASSIST**—to give support or help
- **HELP**—performing an act that lightens someone's load; to aid or assist someone
- **ESTEEM**—the regard in which one is held; *especially* high regard

Application: To demonstrate true humility by seeking, serving, and protecting the well-being of others.

FROM THE WORD

Be quick to give a meal to the hungry, a bed to the homeless—cheerfully. Be generous with the different things God gave you, passing them around so all get in on it. —**1 Peter 4:9-10, MSG**

DEFINE

What does "service" mean to you?

____

____

____

____

____

QUESTIONS 2 PONDER

1. In what ways do you enjoy being served?
2. Do you think that service and sacrifice are the same thing? Why or why not?
3. Is service a requirement?

JUST 4 FUN

Volunteer in a soup kitchen or food pantry with your Guide and afterward discuss how it made you feel to serve those who are financially less fortunate. Brainstorm ways in which you can offer your life to serve those around you and discuss these with your Guide or group.

HERE 2 HELP

Serving comes in a variety of forms. It might be as simple as offering an encouraging word. Or service could be as extensive as helping other kids with a parking-lot trash pickup one Saturday morning. It could mean going on a missions trip to help those who don't have clean water or enough food. It may even mean sacrificing your life so others can live.

Jesus came to give us life, and He asks us to serve others daily. In fact, God created you to do "good works." We read in Ephesians, "We are God's creation. He created us to belong to Christ Jesus. Now we can do good works. Long ago God prepared these works for us to do." (2:10). If you ever wonder why you're here, you have your answer right there: to do good. A "good work" involves an action or activity that benefits others. Good works bring glory to God.

You're here to serve and bring good to those around you. Those people could be your baby sister, parents, friends, teachers, or strangers who live halfway around the world. Doing "good works" for God is a critical reason why you're here.

A servant attitude comes from the heart and ought to be a way of life—a mind-set. The right heart attitude for service is expecting nothing in return. Service is not based on feelings. It's based on simply doing what you were put here to do.

Helping someone else and then expecting something in return is called business, not service. While there is nothing wrong with running a business, you need to understand that it is only service when it is done to glorify God and help someone else. No matter how big or small the action, when it's accompanied by the right spirit of service, God takes notice. He created you for a life of greatness, and that greatness comes by walking the path of service.

IT'S UP 2 YOU

Read each statement. Then select the response that best describes your thoughts and attitudes regarding serving others. Circle the corresponding letter. Follow the directions on tallying your score at the end of the quiz. Ask your Guide for help if you have questions.

1. My family serves the community together.
   A. YES, WE DO THAT OFTEN.
   B. YES, WE HAVE DONE THAT A FEW TIMES.
   C. WE DID THAT ONCE, AND IT WAS HARD WORK.
   D. NO, WE'VE NEVER DONE ANYTHING LIKE THAT.

2. When I have served others it made me feel . . .
   A. SCARED.
   B. TIRED, DIRTY, AND HUNGRY.
   C. A AND B, BUT IT WAS FUN!
   D. FULFILLED AND HAPPY–I COULDN'T WAIT TO DO IT AGAIN.

3. If I see someone who could use help, I help without being asked.
   A. YES, OFTEN
   B. YES, ESPECIALLY IF THEY ARE ELDERLY OR DISABLED
   C. I THINK ABOUT IT, BUT I'M EMBARRASSED TO TRY.
   D. NO, IT'S NOT MY BUSINESS.

4. Earning money for things I want is partially my responsibility.
   A. TRUE, AND I EARN MY OWN MONEY.
   B. I THINK THIS IS TRUE, BUT I DON'T DO IT.
   C. I HAVEN'T THOUGHT ABOUT THIS.
   D. NO, THAT'S WHAT PARENTS AND RELATIVES ARE FOR.

5. I follow Jesus by serving others.
   A. NO, PEOPLE SHOULD HELP THEMSELVES.
   B. NO, MY RELATIONSHIP WITH JESUS IS INSIDE–IT DOESN'T MATTER WHAT I DO.
   C. I SERVE BECAUSE MY PARENTS AND YOUTH LEADER MAKE ME.
   D. YES. HELPING OTHERS IS A WAY TO SHOW LOVE AND COMPASSION.

6. When I serve, I expect nothing in return.
   A. TRUE. IF YOU'RE EXPECTING SOMETHING IN RETURN, THAT ISN'T SERVICE.
   B. TRUE, BUT SOMETIMES PEOPLE DO GIVE YOU SOMETHING AND THAT MAKES THEM FEEL GOOD.
   C. I KNOW I SHOULDN'T EXPECT ANYTHING, BUT I'M HOPEFUL.
   D. IT'S IMPORTANT TO SERVE BECAUSE YOU GET REWARDS AND RECOGNITION.

7. There are plenty of people, even the government, who can help the poor better than I can.
   A. TRUE. THAT'S WHAT THE GOVERNMENT AND CHARITIES ARE FOR.
   B. TRUE. THERE'S NOT MUCH I CAN DO TO MAKE A DIFFERENCE.
   C. I COULD PROBABLY HELP, BUT NO ONE HAS ASKED ME TO GET INVOLVED.
   D. TRUE, BUT I CAN MAKE A BIG DIFFERENCE IN SOMEONE ELSE'S LIFE.

8. When someone else serves me, I feel . . .
   A. HUMBLED AND GRATEFUL; IT MAKES ME WANT TO GIVE BACK.
   B. HUMBLED AND THANKFUL, BUT I WANT TO CRAWL IN A HOLE AND HIDE.
   C. RELIEVED. IT'S ABOUT TIME SOMEONE SAW MY NEED AND HELPED.
   D. EMBARRASSED AND A LITTLE ANGRY. I DON'T WANT OR NEED HELP.

9. Someone, from church/school, asked me to help with a service project.
   A. YES, AND I DID IT AND LOVED IT!
   B. YES, AND I DID IT BECAUSE WE HAVE A COMMUNITY SERVICE REQUIREMENT AT SCHOOL.
   C. YES. I THOUGHT ABOUT IT AND DECIDED NOT TO DO IT.
   D. NO, I'VE NEVER BEEN ASKED TO SERVE.

10. I already know whom I like to serve and the ways I like to serve.
    A. TRUE. I HOPE TO SERVE MORE IN THE FUTURE.
    B. I LOVE TO SERVE, BUT I HAVEN'T IDENTIFIED WHICH WAYS I BEST LIKE TO SERVE.
    C. NOT REALLY. I SERVE BECAUSE IT'S EXPECTED OF ME.
    D. NO, I RARELY SERVE.

IT'S UP 2 YOU (CONTINUED)

SERVICE SCORECARD

For each question, assign the following point values for the answer chosen. Then total the number of points you have on the assessment.

1. Answer:	A-5	B-4	C-3	D-2	POINTS:
2. Answer:	A-2	B-3	C-4	D-5	POINTS:
3. Answer:	A-5	B-4	C-3	D-2	POINTS:
4. Answer:	A-5	B-4	C-3	D-2	POINTS:
5. Answer:	A-2	B-3	C-4	D-5	POINTS:
6. Answer:	A-5	B-4	C-3	D-2	POINTS:
7. Answer:	A-2	B-3	C-4	D-5	POINTS:
8. Answer:	A-5	B-4	C-3	D-2	POINTS:
9. Answer:	A-5	B-4	C-3	D-2	POINTS:
10. Answer:	A-5	B-4	C-3	D-2	POINTS:

TOTAL POINTS:

SERVICE PROFILE

If your total points score was . . .

40–50: You have already benefited from serving. Your soul—your mind, will, and emotions—are stronger for the experience. Thank the adults in your life who made these opportunities possible. If the Lord has given you a vision for serving others, go after it with a whole heart.

30–39: You have experienced some of the benefits of serving. Consider spending more time serving; there's probably some activity you can give up to make time for it. Ask your Guide for ways he/she thinks you need to grow in serving others. Also pray and ask God to show you why your heart may be hard in those areas. Read the Beatitudes (Matthew 5:1-12) to discover the blessings Jesus has for you through service.

20–29: God desires for you to get out of your comfort zone and start serving. Service is sure to stir your heart in powerful ways. If your first experiences don't deliver on this, keep searching for an opportunity that will. If your family is not serving, you can be the one to make service a priority in your home. Through prayer, ask the Lord to move your mind-set toward becoming a giver.

MEANING

Belief that someone or something is reliable, good, honest, and effective.

TRUST

- **CONFIDENCE**—certain of trustworthiness
- **FAITH**—confident belief
- **RELIABLE**—likely to be true or correct

Application: Someone may have let you down in the past. Perhaps your ability to trust people is fragile. But God still wants you to learn how to find trustworthy people and learn to trust them.

FROM THE WORD

Sovereign LORD, you are God! Your words are trustworthy, and you have promised good things to your servant. **—2 Samuel 7:28, NIV**

This key lesson was developed by Doug Schmidt, Peacemakers Ministry.

DEFINE

What does "trust" mean to you?

QUESTIONS 2 PONDER

1. Who are the three people you trust most?
2. What would cause you to trust or distrust someone?
3. Can your friends count on you to keep a secret? In other words, are *you* trustworthy?

JUST 4 FUN

Read the story below and then discuss the following questions.

THE FROG AND THE SCORPION

One day a frog was sunbathing on the bank of a small pond. Suddenly, he saw a scorpion approaching. The frog had seen scorpions sting other frogs, and so he cautiously started moving away.

"Don't go," said the scorpion. "I come to ask a simple favor. I need a ride to the other side of the pond—on your back."

The frog nearly croaked. "Are you kidding?" he asked. "You'll stab me in the back, and then I'll drown!"

"Why, we'd both drown if I were to do something as foolish as that," said the scorpion.

Convinced the scorpion's motives were pure, the frog let the scorpion creep onto its back. They began making their way across the pond.

When they were a few feet out, the frog felt a sudden piercing pain in his back. The frog's limbs began to go numb.

As they were both sinking, the frog asked, "Why did you stab me in the back with your poisonous tail?"

The scorpion replied, "Hmmm, I guess it's just my nature."

1. What was the frog's previous experience with scorpions?
2. How did the scorpion convince the frog to take him across the pond?
3. What was the scorpion's reason for stinging the frog, even though they would both die?
4. Do you believe that people will always act "according to their nature"? Explain.
5. Why is it often hard for those who have been stung in the past to trust *anyone*?
6. After you've been let down, does God expect you to try trusting again?

HERE 2 HELP

Learning to lean on trustworthy people is one of the most valuable skills you can get into your "relationship tool-box." Of course, to trust at any level requires a degree of risk. If you've been disappointed in the past, it's even riskier. But with a little practice, you'll be able to figure out the best people to trust.

You *can* find those trustworthy people. One way to do this is to start a conversation. During that talk, you intentionally tell the other person why you did a particular thing or attempted something new. Say something like "I dyed my hair green to try out for the *Willy Wonka* play at school. I want to be an oompa loompa."

Notice how the other person reacts to your idea.

If he or she says something like "Wow, that was really stupid—what were you thinking?" then you have a clue that person is critical. You probably want to step back from trusting that person too much. On the other hand, if the person affirms you—"Wow, that shows total commitment. I hope you get the role!"—or respectfully makes suggestions—"What's your timeline for changing it back to your natural color?"—well, maybe you've found yourself a winner there.

Practice having these types of conversations with your Guide. Swap roles and practice becoming an affirming person. It's important not only to find trustworthy, safe people, but also to become one.

IT'S UP 2 YOU

In the first column of the table below, name ten people in your life whom you know fairly well and who know you.

NAME	TRUST LEVEL	WHY?

On a scale of 1 to 10 (10 meaning the highest confidence possible), at what level would you trust each of these people? Put that number in the "Trust Level" column for each person. Then in the "Why?" column, put down a brief explanation about why you put that particular number. Is it low because that person tends to be a gossip? Is it high because that person is always kind to you, even when you mess up? How much variation is there in the numbers? Do you tend to trust everyone at the same level? Or do you trust no one at all?

Here are some questions that you might be able to answer by calling 1-800-CAPTAIN-OBVIOUS, but they are worth asking anyway. Why is it wise to keep trustworthy people close to you—and the less-than-trustworthy a bit further away? What can happen if we trust the wrong people? What can happen if we refuse to trust safe people?

LEVEL IV
MY BRAND

KINGDOM KEY 10

COMMUNICATION

GOALS

1. You will learn the key components of good communication.
2. You will discover what communication is appropriate for social media.
3. You will discuss the distraction of electronics in face-to-face communication.

MEANING

The act or process of using words, sounds, signs, or behaviors to express or exchange information or to express your ideas, thoughts, and feelings to someone else

- **NONVERBAL**—communicating without using words
- **TALK**—to say words in order to express your thoughts, feelings, or opinions to someone
- **LISTEN**—to hear what someone has said and seek to understand it

Biblical Meaning: Interacting with another in a respectful and timely fashion.

FROM THE WORD

Don't let any evil talk come out of your mouths. Say only what will help to build others up and meet their needs. Then what you say will help those who listen. **—Ephesians 4:29**

DEFINE

What does "communication" mean to you?

QUESTIONS 2 PONDER

1. What is your favorite way to communicate?
2. In what ways can certain forms of communication hurt someone?
3. Why is communication an important part of being a Christian?

JUST 4 FUN

It's important to choose your words wisely and share only the communication that is best for any situation. The following task will help you learn what is appropriate to share on social media or in groups.

1. First gather a large white T-shirt, a Sharpie or permanent marker, and some small pieces of paper.
2. Brainstorm with your group about the topics discussed on social media or when you're with a group of trusted friends, like in a baseball/softball dugout, Sunday school, or a slumber party. Capture everything from friendships, family life, and daily activities.
3. After you collect a list with at least eight items, decide which topics you would normally share with everybody on social media. Then decide which topics you would talk about only privately with a close friend. On the white T-shirt, write those specific topics you'd share on social media or with most anyone. Write the remaining topics you should avoid sharing on the small pieces of paper. Place them in a jar. When the activity is over, have someone wear the T-shirt.

It's important to understand that social media and sharing in groups is public and permanent. Online, everyone will know and always have access to the information you share. Choosing to keep some things "under a lid" is wise. Those private conversations and topics can be contained and shared with those closest to you.

HERE 2 HELP

Have you ever been talking with someone and felt as if he or she wasn't listening? Perhaps you saw his or her eyes wander. You could tell this person's mind was thinking about something else. When you were finished talking, did he or she change the subject? How did you feel when that happened? Hurt? Angry?

Have you ever told someone about a great experience, but the other person didn't pay attention? Worse yet, this person just kept talking about him- or herself?

Those were times of unhealthy communication. Healthy communication happens when one person shares something and the other person understands and responds. This doesn't mean that the other person has to agree. But it does mean that he or she at least listens and communicates something back to show understanding.

This process is called *validation*. To validate means you recognize the importance of what was communicated. This comes out of a respectful heart for the other person. It's your way of saying that even if you don't agree, you respect the way the other person feels or views something.

List three or four ways you can validate someone who is talking to you:

____

____

____

Think of a few people you know who listen to you. What do they do to make you feel "heard"?

____

____

____

IT'S UP 2 YOU

There are three parts in communication.

1. The *encoder* is the person who wants to say something.

2. The *message* is what's actually said and includes the emotion behind it.

3. The *decoder* receives and deciphers the message to make sense of it.

With a partner or your Guide, take turns encoding and decoding messages. You'll see that the decoder is not passive. He or she needs to ask questions about the message, and then retell the message, including a summary of the details, what the encoder thought about the message, and how the encoder felt about the message.

Suggested topics for the encoder:

- Tell about your favorite birthday
- Describe an argument or disagreement you've had with a family member
- Tell about a time when you saw someone do something brave

Sample questions for the decoder:

- How did you feel during your special birthday party?
- When did the disagreement take place? Are you still angry?
- Why do you think the brave person did that?

QUESTIONS ABOUT COMMUNICATION

Answer these questions to learn more about effective communication:

1. Would you consider yourself a better listener (decoder) or talker (encoder)? Why? Give an example.

___

___

___

2. Why is decoding important in any conversation?

___

___

___

3. Say (encode) the following statements to a partner in such a way that they are positive. Ask the listener (decoder) to tell what your meaning is. Then repeat the statement, and by changing your tone and nonverbal signals, see if you change the meaning of each statement. Then discuss the importance of tone and body language as it relates to communication.

   a. "I can't believe it! The [fill in a sports team] won."
   b. "Spaghetti for dinner again!"
   c. "That dress is sure eye-catching."
   d. "I hope he gets everything he deserves."

IT'S UP 2 YOU (CONTINUED)

QUESTIONS ABOUT ELECTRONIC DEVICES

Answer the following questions:

1. Would you say that kids can be good encoders if they are distracted by electronics (games, phones, computers)?
2. If you didn't use electronics during long car rides, what would happen?
3. In what ways do electronic devices hinder kids from communicating with others?

KINGDOM KEY 11
TEAMWORK

GOALS

1. You will learn what unity means.
2. You will practice working together on a common goal.
3. You will discover your teamwork profile.

MEANING

The work accomplished by people acting together as a team; unity

TEAMWORK

- **UNITY**—being in full agreement; a balanced, pleasing, or suitable grouping of parts
- **COOPERATE**—to work with another person or group to do something
- **SYNERGY**—the improved results when two or more people work together

Application: To work in harmony toward a shared purpose and vision.

FROM THE WORD

[Be] diligent to preserve the unity of the Spirit in the bond of peace.
—Ephesians 4:3, NASB

DEFINE

What does "teamwork" mean to you?

____

____

____

____

____

QUESTIONS 2 PONDER

1. Are you a team player? Explain your answer.
2. Do you think that things are easier or harder when you are part of a team?
3. Was Jesus part of a team?

JUST 4 FUN

This activity, called Group Project, requires more than one person. For each person, gather a soft fabric scrap about two feet long and two inches wide, or gather one large rubber band for each person. Have the group members stand side-by-side in a circle; each person should face inward. Using the fabric scrap or large rubber band, connect each person's right wrist to the left wrist of the person next to him or her. Make sure the fabric or rubber band is not too tight. Leave the last two wrists free so the circle isn't closed.

Choose a task to do together as a group while you're connected. The task could be making a sandwich, rearranging the furniture in a room, or wrapping a present. In this process, you'll discover that each person who is part of a larger group must come together in order to accomplish the goal.

YOUR WORK IS PRODUCED BY YOUR FAITH. YOUR SERVICE IS THE RESULT OF YOUR LOVE. YOUR STRENGTH TO CONTINUE COMES FROM YOUR HOPE IN OUR LORD JESUS CHRIST.

1 THESSALONIANS 1:3

HERE 2 HELP

Everyone has heard the phrase, "There is no *I* in *TEAM*." In team sports one individual does not determine the outcome of a game. The teammates contribute too. No matter how good an individual player is at his or her particular sport, how much desire he or she has to win, or how hard he or she works during the game, if the team isn't involved, that individual will usually experience a loss. Wins and losses in team sports are determined by the strong, cohesive effort of the team, not the ability of an individual player.

One of the reasons people experience loss and failure in life is that they aren't surrounded by people with the same goals. They don't have people around them who also want to live by the Bible's standards.

Most people try to live life independently, keeping control as an individual. However, life is best lived as a team.

These teammates want to help you grow up to be a godly person. Therefore, your wins and losses in life are determined by the efforts of your team. They are not determined by your individual ability and efforts.

In life, like in sports, we need to have unity as a team. However, unity does *not* mean uniformity. Not everyone is alike.

What if everyone who made up your favorite sports team played the same position? That wouldn't make for a good team! Or think about your favorite music group. What if everyone played the same instrument and the same notes? That music group wouldn't be worth listening to.

The definition of unity is working together toward a shared purpose. Each person should bring his or her own unique skills and personality to the team. That way the group becomes stronger than it would without that person.

TWO PEOPLE ARE BETTER THAN ONE. THEY CAN HELP EACH OTHER IN EVERYTHING THEY DO.

ECCLESIASTES 4:9

IT'S UP 2 YOU

Read each statement. Then select the response that best describes your interactions with others. Circle the corresponding letter. Follow the directions on tallying your score at the end of the quiz. Ask your Guide for help if you have questions.

1. When I work in a group, I listen carefully to what other team members say.
   A. ALWAYS
   B. MOST OF THE TIME
   C. MY MIND DRIFTS WHEN I'M IN A GROUP.
   D. I DON'T HAVE TIME FOR THAT.

2. I get upset when my team takes credit for my idea or action, and I don't get recognition.
   A. ALWAYS
   B. MOST OF THE TIME
   C. SELDOM. IT'S MEETING THE GOAL.
   D. NEVER. IT REALLY DOESN'T MATTER WHOSE IDEA IT WAS.

3. If one of my friends is offended, I am offended too.
   A. ALWAYS, AND I LET OTHERS KNOW ABOUT IT.
   B. USUALLY, AND I LET IT AFFECT HOW I TREAT THE OFFENDER.
   C. SOMETIMES, BUT I TRY TO HELP THEM RECONCILE.
   D. NEVER

4. If I'm in conflict with someone, I make sure to avoid him or her whenever possible.
   A. ALWAYS
   B. MOST OF THE TIME
   C. I DO, UNTIL I'M READY TO TALK ABOUT THE ISSUE.
   D. NEVER. I STARE DOWN OR TELL THAT PERSON HE OR SHE IS WRONG.

5. When I'm upset with someone, I tell others about it.
   A. YES, ESPECIALLY IF I KNOW THEY'LL BE ON MY SIDE.
   B. MOST OF THE TIME—I NEED TO LET IT OUT.
   C. SELDOM, OR ONLY WITH FRIENDS I TRUST TO HELP ME SORT IT OUT.
   D. NEVER. I KEEP NEGATIVE THINGS TO MYSELF AND KEEP GOING.

6. When I'm upset with someone, I check my attitude before confronting him or her about it.
   A. ALWAYS
   B. MOST OF THE TIME
   C. SELDOM; IT'S A LOT OF WORK TO THINK ABOUT IT.
   D. I'M NEVER WRONG, AND IT'S PROBABLY THE OTHER PERSON'S FAULT ANYWAY.

7. If someone wrongs me, I'm not satisfied until I have had a chance to get even.
   A. TRUE, THE BIBLE SAYS, "AN EYE FOR AN EYE."
   B. IT DEPENDS ON WHAT THE PERSON DID.
   C. SOMETIMES I FEEL THAT WAY, BUT THEY'LL GET THEIRS IN THE END.
   D. I TRY TO OVERLOOK IT AND MOVE ON.

8. Sometimes I pretend that things others say or do don't bother me, even when my feelings are hurt or I'm angry.
   A. YES, I DO THIS OFTEN.
   B. YES, WITH SOME PEOPLE
   C. NOT REALLY—I LIKE TO WORK IT OUT.
   D. IT'S PRETTY DIFFICULT TO HURT MY FEELINGS.

9. If I'm in conflict with someone, I check myself for what responsibility I might have.
   A. ALWAYS. CONFLICT TAKES AT LEAST TWO.
   B. MOST OF THE TIME
   C. SELDOM OR NEVER—IT'S IMPORTANT TO TELL THE OTHER PERSON WHAT THEY DID WRONG.
   D. SELDOM OR NEVER—I AVOID CONFLICT AT ALL COSTS.

10. It's really important to resolve conflict. I like to be at peace within myself and with others.
   A. STRONGLY AGREE
   B. AGREE
   C. DISAGREE
   D. STRONGLY DISAGREE

IT'S UP 2 YOU (CONTINUED)

TEAMWORK SCORECARD

For each question, assign the following Response Value for the answer chosen. The three Response Values are

E—Escape Response
A—Attack Response
P—Peacemaking Response

Tally the number of similar responses at the bottom of the scorecard to discover if you respond to conflict using mostly Escape Responses (E), Attack Responses (A), or Peacemaking Responses (P).

1. Answer:	A=P	B=P	C=E	D=A	RESPONSE:
2. Answer:	A=A	B=A	C=P	D=E	RESPONSE:
3. Answer:	A=A	B=A	C=P	D=E	RESPONSE:
4. Answer:	A=E	B=E	C=P	D=A	RESPONSE:
5. Answer:	A=A	B=A	C=P	D=E	RESPONSE:
6. Answer:	A=P	B=P	C=E	D=A	RESPONSE:
7. Answer:	A=A	B=A	C=E	D=P	RESPONSE:
8. Answer:	A=E	B=E	C=P	D=A	RESPONSE:
9. Answer:	A=P	B=P	C=A	D=E	RESPONSE:
10. Answer:	A=P	B=P	C=E AND A	D=E AND A	RESPONSE:

TOTAL ESCAPE RESPONSES: ☐

TOTAL ATTACK RESPONSES: ☐

TOTAL PEACEMAKING RESPONSES: ☐

TEAMWORK PROFILE

If your score was above three points in the Escape Response or Attack Response totals, read on. It's time to consider your role in conflict with others. Romans 12:17-18 advises us to avoid revenge: "Don't pay back evil with evil. Be careful to do what everyone thinks is right. If possible, live in peace with everyone. Do that as much as you can."

The verse also encourages us to find ways to live at peace with others. We're charged with the task of resolving conflict. On the other hand, while some offenses can be overlooked, others must be reconciled so we don't harbor anger, pain, guilt, or other negative emotions. Those can build up until they reach a boiling point. Our goal is to be peacemakers.

If you've fallen into habits of escaping or attacking, it will take discipline to learn to be a peacemaker. The rewards of being a peacemaker—inner peace, less stress and frustration, and peace with others—will be well worth it.

KINGDOM KEY 12

RESPECT

GOALS

1. You will create a personal crest reflecting your values and who you are.
2. You will identify ways to show respect to yourself and others.
3. You will take a quiz to find out how respectful you are.

MEANING

An act of giving particular attention; high or special regard.

RESPECT

- **HONOR**—quality treatment that is given to someone or something
- **REGARD**—care or concern at a high level for someone or something
- **CONSIDERATION**—caring about other people's feelings, wants, or needs

Application: Respect involves more than action; it includes the heart because out of the heart comes the action. It begins with self-respect—viewing yourself the way God sees you.

FROM THE WORD

Show proper respect to everyone. Love the family of believers. Have respect for God. Honor the [government]. **—I Peter 2:17**

DEFINE

What does "respect" mean to you?

QUESTIONS 2 PONDER

1. Do you think that people in our society show enough respect?
2. Whom do you respect and why?
3. Have you ever been disrespected? How did it make you feel?

JUST 4 FUN

Create your own personal crest either by drawing it, using your computer or tablet, or cutting and pasting pictures from magazines or newspapers. You'll have to chose which things you will use to represent yourself, your family, and your personal history. You can also include something that shows who you want to be as an adult.

This activity is designed to show respect to your family—even if your parents don't live in the same house—so think of the good or special things that set your family apart: your last name, things you do well, etc.

JUST 4 FUN (CONTINUED)

It's also meant to show respect to yourself and your future. Choose symbols of goals that you'd like to reach or character qualities you want to be known for and represent them in your crest.

In the medieval ages when a knight was given a specific honor, his family crest (coat of arms) was displayed throughout the town as a symbol of honor. What do you consider highly respectable about yourself?

HERE 2 HELP

Here are practical ways to respect yourself and others. See how many you're already doing:

- ☐ Value others' opinions and presence.
- ☐ Don't interrupt someone when he or she is talking.
- ☐ Don't be disagreeable just for the sake of disagreeing.
- ☐ Seek to understand someone else's perspective, even if it differs from yours.

LOVE FROM THE CENTER OF WHO YOU ARE; DON'T FAKE IT. . . . BE GOOD FRIENDS WHO LOVE DEEPLY; PRACTICE PLAYING SECOND FIDDLE.

ROMANS 12:9-10, MSG

HERE 2 HELP (CONTINUED)

- ☐ Fulfill your responsibilities in relationship to others. (Put your own trash or dishes away; clean shared living spaces; be on time and don't make other people wait for you; submit homework on time, etc.)
- ☐ Don't talk too loudly so as to draw attention to yourself.
- ☐ Be courteous and practice good manners.
- ☐ Make eye contact when you're talking with others. (Don't look at your phone or tablet.)
- ☐ Chew gum with your mouth closed. Better yet, don't chew gum in public.
- ☐ Be neat in your appearance.
- ☐ Don't dominate conversations.
- ☐ Offer the elderly your seat at a restaurant lobby or on a bus or subway.
- ☐ Don't use harmful and/or illegal things such as alcohol or drugs/cigarettes.
- ☐ Speak well of yourself and don't put yourself down in conversation.
- ☐ Spend time in God's Word to grow in wisdom and make good choices.
- ☐ Eat healthful foods and limit junk food.
- ☐ Exercise.

Identify five ways that were not mentioned in which you can show respect either to yourself or others:

____

____

____

____

____

____

____

IT'S UP 2 YOU

Read each statement. Decide which response best describes your thoughts and opinions about respect. Circle the corresponding letter. Follow the directions on tallying your score at the end of the quiz. Ask your Guide for help if you have questions.

1. I take good care of myself—spirit, mind, and body.
   A. ALWAYS
   B. MOST OF THE TIME
   C. NOT REALLY
   D. I SAY, IF IT FEELS GOOD, DO IT.

2. I do not enter into conversations that I consider to be disrespectful.
   A. TRUE
   B. I USUALLY STEER CLEAR OF THOSE SITUATIONS.
   C. IT DEPENDS ON THE TOPIC AND WHO IS TALKING.
   D. WHAT'S THE DIFFERENCE?

3. Respect should be given only when deserved or earned.
   A. STRONGLY AGREE-IF YOU RESPECT ME, THEN I WILL RESPECT YOU.
   B. AGREE
   C. DISAGREE-YOU SHOULD ACT RESPECTFULLY EVEN IF YOU DON'T FEEL IT.
   D. STRONGLY DISAGREE-ALL PEOPLE DESERVE RESPECT AT ALL TIMES.

4. I have an adult role model—parent or mentor or coach or teacher—who treats me with respect.
   A. YES, I HAVE SEVERAL.
   B. YES, A FEW
   C. YES, I CAN THINK OF ONE.
   D. NO, I DON'T.

5. My school has an atmosphere that is respectful toward all people.
   A. STRONGLY AGREE
   B. AGREE
   C. DISAGREE
   D. STRONGLY DISAGREE

IT'S UP 2 YOU (CONTINUED)

6. Treating other people with respect is very important to me.
   A. ALWAYS
   B. MOST OF THE TIME
   C. SOMETIMES
   D. NO, IT DOESN'T MATTER TO ME.

7. It's very important that others treat me with respect.
   A. ALWAYS
   B. MOST OF THE TIME
   C. SOMETIMES
   D. NO, IT DOESN'T MATTER TO ME.

8. There is nothing wrong with using electronics while someone is talking to me.
   A. TRUE
   B. MOST OF THE TIME
   C. IT DEPENDS ON WHO IS TALKING.
   D. NO, PEOPLE DESERVE MY FULL ATTENTION.

9. It's easy for me to listen and make eye contact.
   A. TRUE
   B. MOST OF THE TIME
   C. IT DEPENDS ON WHO I'M WITH.
   D. NO, I'M UNCOMFORTABLE GIVING OR RECEIVING THAT MUCH ATTENTION.

10. My opinion of what is or isn't respectful is more important than anyone else's.
    A. STRONGLY AGREE
    B. AGREE
    C. DISAGREE
    D. STRONGLY DISAGREE

RESPECT SCORECARD

For each question, assign the following Sensitivity Value (High Sensitivity, Medium Sensitivity, or Low Sensitivity) for the answer chosen. Tally the number of similar responses at the bottom of the scorecard. If you don't understand how to do this, ask your Guide for help.

1. Answer:	A=H	B=M	C=L	D=L	SENSITIVITY:
2. Answer:	A=H	B=H	C=M	D=L	SENSITIVITY:
3. Answer:	A=L	B=M	C=M	D=H	SENSITIVITY:
4. Answer:	A=H	B=M	C=M	D=L	SENSITIVITY:
5. Answer:	A=M	B=M	C=L	D=H	SENSITIVITY:
6. Answer:	A=H	B=H	C=M	D=L	SENSITIVITY:
7. Answer:	A=H	B=H	C=M	D=L	SENSITIVITY:
8. Answer:	A=L	B=L	C=L	D=H	SENSITIVITY:
9. Answer:	A=H	B=H	C=M	D=L	SENSITIVITY:
10. Answer:	A=L	B=L	C=M	D=H	SENSITIVITY:

TOTAL HIGH SENSITIVITY RESPONSES: ☐

TOTAL MEDIUM SENSITIVITY RESPONSES: ☐

TOTAL LOW SENSITIVITY RESPONSES: ☐

These totals will show you areas in which you may need to grow. Go back to any (L) low- or (M) medium-sensitivity responses you marked and discuss those with your Guide.

WHOEVER HAS RESPECT FOR THE LORD LIVES A GOOD LIFE.

PROVERBS 14:2

LEVEL V
MY NEXT LEVEL

KINGDOM KEY 13
PURPOSE

GOALS

1. You will be able to identify your spiritual gifts.
2. You will discover the strengths and weaknesses of your life experiences and how they relate to purpose.
3. You will learn the different ingredients that make up a person's purpose.

MEANING

The aim or goal of a person; what a person is trying to do or become

- **DESIGN**—to be made for a specific function or end
- **DESTINY**—something a person or thing is intended to fulfill
- **MEANING**—the reason something or someone is planned to be

Application: Your purpose is the customized life-calling God chose for you. He has things for you to accomplish that will bring Him glory and expand His kingdom.

FROM THE WORD

I cry out to God Most High, to God who fulfills his purpose for me.
—Psalm 57:2, ESV

DEFINE

What does "purpose" mean to you?

____

____

____

____

____

QUESTIONS 2 PONDER

1. What role does your background play in your purpose?
2. Can a person have more than one purpose? Explain.
3. What things can you do to prepare for your future even if you don't know your purpose?
4. Do you think a person's purpose has a time limit? Can a person miss his or her chance?

JUST 4 FUN

Choose a favorite dessert and collect the ingredients to bake together with your Guide and/or fellow soldiers. Talk about the importance of using the right ingredients and measurements. Discuss how using too much baking soda will cause the dessert to be bitter or too much sugar will make it syrupy and too sweet.

JUST 4 FUN (CONTINUED)

While you're cooking, discuss what you think your spiritual gifts are. A spiritual gifts assessment to discover your personal gifts will be offered in the It's Up 2 You section. On the following line(s), write what you think your gifts are. After you take the assessment, you can compare your prediction with your actual outcome.

____

____

How do you think those gifts will help you fulfill your life's purpose?

____

____

DAVID, AFTER HE HAD SERVED THE PURPOSE OF GOD IN HIS OWN GENERATION, FELL ASLEEP.

ACTS 13:36, ESV

HERE 2 HELP

Your purpose is unique to you—just like your fingerprints. Answer the following questions about your passion, skills, and personality to find out more about your purpose.

PASSION

What energizes you? What job would you want even if you didn't get paid? What excites you?

Pay attention when those answers line up with ways to help others. Your passion will involve something that keeps you living out your purpose when life gets boring or involves conflict and struggle. Your passion brings fulfillment and gives you the determination to move forward.

SKILLS

What are you good at? Which skills/talents do people compliment you about? What types of things do people look toward you to do?

PERSONALITY

Do you like to be with people, or do you prefer to have alone time? Are you a go-getter or are you more cautious? Do you enjoy leading or following? Do you work better by yourself or with other people?

Your personality is a great indicator of what God designed you to do because it reflects His purpose for you. Has He given you a personality that makes you enjoy being with people and talking a lot? If so, then look where those traits line up with various purposes/occupations such as teaching, counseling, or speaking. Your personality can help determine what will be the best fit for you long-term in a career and in your relationships.

When you combine your passion, skills, and personality, see where they link up. Then you're on your way to discovering your purpose.

IT'S UP 2 YOU

A great way to discover your spiritual gifts is to take a spiritual gifts inventory. Here's one created by Focus on the Family counselor and author Tim Sanford.

Work through all seven lists. Mark an XX by any statements that seem to fit you *well.* Mark with a single X the statements you think *may* fit you.

When you've completed all six lists, add up the statements you marked on each list and enter that number at the end of the list. Give yourself one point for each statement, whether you marked it XX or only X.

You'll probably find that one or two lists have more statements marked than the others. Those lists may indicate your spiritual gift(s). Don't be surprised if more than one list has lots of marks. You may have two gifts—a primary gift and a secondary gift.

SPIRITUAL GIFTS INVENTORY

LIST 1

____ You're confident when you talk to others.

____ You tend to remember Bible stories and verses. You can explain Bible truths to others.

____ Feelings don't matter as much to you as facts and truth do.

____ You tend to do more talking than listening.

____ You strongly believe that people should respect God.

____ You have strong opinions and sometimes others call you stubborn.

____ **Total number of statements you marked out of 6**

LIST 2

____ You care about the details of what needs to be done.

____ You find it hard to say no when something needs to be done.

____ You want to get the job over with so you can get to the next one.

____ You listen to others without criticizing them.

____ You're comfortable with letting others be in charge.

____ You can put up with people who might irritate others.

____ **Total number of statements you marked out of 6**

LIST 3

_____ You like learning and helping others learn.

_____ You like arranging facts in a simple way so others can remember them.

_____ You like to quote the Bible and other sources to support what you say.

_____ It's easy for you to become proud of your knowledge.

_____ You're self-disciplined.

_____ You make decisions based on facts.

_____ **Total number of statements you marked out of 6**

LIST 4

_____ Nearly everything you do is practical.

_____ You believe that with God, *anything* is possible.

_____ You like helping others solve their problems.

_____ It's hard for you to accept failure.

_____ You find success exciting.

_____ You tend to give people advice instead of just befriending them.

_____ **Total number of statements you marked out of 6**

LIST 5

_____ You insist that people follow the rules.

_____ You're confident and comfortable being a leader.

_____ You're good at organizing and details.

_____ You're able to sit quietly and listen before making comments.

_____ You thrive on pressure—the more the better.

_____ You tend to accept others based on loyalty or ability to finish a task.

_____ **Total number of statements you marked out of 6**

LIST 6

_____ You're very sensitive to others' feelings.

_____ You're patient and will go to great lengths to help others.

_____ You find it tough to be firm with others.

_____ You will give a lot to lessen others' pain and suffering.

_____ You talk well with people, and they find it easy to talk to you.

_____ When it comes to getting along with others, you can put up with a lot.

_____ **Total number of statements you marked out of 6**

IT'S UP 2 YOU (CONTINUED)

DOWN TO EARTH

Take a look at the totals of each list. Does one list have more marks than the others? If so, that may be your primary spiritual gift. Does a second list stand out above the remaining five? That may be a secondary gift.

If no list stands out, look over the descriptions and see if one fits you better than the rest. Keep in mind that other issues, including stress, may block your ability to see a spiritual gift—and could block a gift from being displayed at all. So be patient, and come back to this exercise later if necessary.

This test looks for six of what have been called the "seven motivational gifts" in Romans 12:3–8. (We cut the one on financial giving because that usually comes later in life.) Here are their descriptions:

LIST 1: PROPHECY

If you have the gift of prophecy, you're probably highly sensitive to whether others are okay spiritually. You may not notice this now, but it may become clear as you mature. Being a prophet doesn't mean you have to hear God's audible voice talking to you; it means you're able to understand God's message.

LIST 2: SERVICE

If you have the gift of service, you want to take care of the practical and physical needs of others. You're good at identifying unmet needs and helping others.

LIST 3: TEACHING

With this gift, you have a passion for the truth and tend to make it clear for others. You can communicate important information as a teacher or coach.

LIST 4: EXHORTATION

People with this gift are often seen as the encouragers or cheerleaders of a group. You can bring comfort and counsel to others.

LIST 5: ADMINISTRATION

If you have this gift, you like getting people to work together toward a goal. When you and your friends are planning a major activity, you're likely the one who gets everyone and everything organized.

LIST 6: MERCY

The gift of mercy is not "feeling sorry" for people. If you have this gift, you have a strong desire to heal physical and/or emotional wounds. You feel compassion for hurting people, and translate that into actions that show love and relieve suffering.

TAKEAWAY

Other gifts may fall under the six categories listed here. For example, the gift of hospitality could fall under the headings of either mercy or service.

Remember, this is not a scientific test with absolute answers. But it does give you a good starting point for considering what your spiritual gift(s) may be.

FORM YOUR PURPOSE BY ASKING FOR COUNSEL, THEN CARRY IT OUT USING ALL THE HELP YOU CAN GET.

PROVERBS 20:18, MSG

KINGDOM KEY 14

RESILIENCE

GOALS

1. You will identify areas in your life that need resiliency.
2. You will learn a plan to enable you to be resilient.
3. You will discover the value of not giving up despite what you might have lost.

MEANING

The ability to become strong, healthy, or successful again after something bad happens; the ability of something to return to its original shape after it has been pulled, stretched, pressed, or bent

RESILIENCE/RESILIENT

- **ADAPTABLE**—able to change or be changed in order to fit or work better; able to adapt or be adapted
- **LITHE**—easily bent; graceful
- **TENACITY**—not easily stopped; strong, continuing for a long time, very determined to do something

Application: When you get knocked down, you can bounce back or get up quickly. You can handle and manage life, stress, change, and even disappointments (setbacks) in a positive and constructive way.

FROM THE WORD

Whatever I have, wherever I am, I can make it through anything in the One who makes me who I am. **—Philippians 4:13, MSG**

DEFINE

What does "resilient" mean to you?

____

____

____

____

____

QUESTIONS 2 PONDER

1. Describe a time when you had to bounce back after being disappointed.
2. When is it okay to feel disappointed?
3. True or False? If you want to be resilient, you have to ignore your feelings. Explain your answer.

JUST 4 FUN

Talk with your Guide about how you'd respond in each of these situations.

1. Your family has to move to a new town in the middle of the school year. That means leaving your friends and your church youth group, and changing your school situation (even if you're homeschooled). What are things you can do to help yourself adjust?
2. While the teacher was out of the classroom, someone said something that wasn't true about you, and all your classmates heard it. (If you're homeschooled, imagine it happened at a sports practice or choir rehearsal.) You didn't have the chance to defend yourself, and now the bell has rung. What will you do?
3. You didn't get a part in the play, a spot on the team, or advanced to the next level in 4-H or martial arts. How do you feel about this? What are your plans?
4. In what areas of life is it difficult for you to handle disappointment? Friendships? Sports? Academics? Family? List the top three areas in your life in which you struggle with disappointment:

____

____

____

____

Discuss with your Guide practical things you can do to better prepare yourself for handling disappointment in each of these three areas.

HERE 2 HELP

Sometimes life isn't fair. Sometimes bad things do happen. Things change. People disappoint you. You disappoint yourself. When that happens, follow these tips for being resilient:

Talk it out. Find a parent, trusted friend, or mentor to talk through what happened and how you feel about the situation. Talk about possible positive ways you can respond or gain a new perspective.

Find your safe space. Sometimes it helps to be in a place where you feel in control. Maybe that's in your room. Determine this safe space and go there to think clearly.

Do something small. When you face a challenge, sometimes everything feels overwhelming. Do something small that makes you feel as if you can accomplish something. Then see if your outlook isn't brighter.

Give yourself a break. We all have setbacks, make mistakes, and get hurt. Sometimes we even respond incorrectly. So give yourself time to recover. Avoid things that stress you and don't tackle anything demanding until you have time to think through the challenge.

Exercise. Exercise is a great way to process stress and clear your mind. It puts you in a position to better handle your response to a stressful situation.

Help someone else. One of the best ways to face life's trials is to help someone else. This takes your focus off of you—and often renews your perspective.

Learn from it, but don't live in it. Think about a car. It has a large glass window in the front. This is for you to see where you're going when you drive. It also has a small rearview mirror so you can see where you've been or what's behind you. When you drive, if you stare in the rearview mirror too long you'll crash. Live your life as if you're driving. Glance back, but don't stare. Learn from challenging circumstances, but don't live in them. Don't crash; instead move forward.

BLESSED IS THE MAN WHO REMAINS STEADFAST UNDER TRIAL, FOR WHEN HE HAS STOOD THE TEST HE WILL RECEIVE THE CROWN OF LIFE, WHICH GOD HAS PROMISED TO THOSE WHO LOVE HIM.

JAMES 1:12, ESV

IT'S UP 2 YOU

Read each statement. Choose the answer that best reflects the way you think about and respond to challenging situations. Circle the corresponding letter. Follow the directions on tallying your score at the end of the quiz. Ask your Guide for help if you have questions.

1. I look at mistakes as an opportunity to learn how to do something better.
   A. ALWAYS B. MOST OF THE TIME C. SOMETIMES D. RARELY

2. I have someone in my life I can count on for encouragement when I'm disappointed.
   A. YES, THERE IS SOMEONE WHO WILL HELP ME OVERCOME HARDSHIPS.
   B. SOMETIMES
   C. SELDOM
   D. NEVER. IT'S UP TO ME TO DECIDE WHETHER OR NOT TO QUIT.

3. When things around me are out of my control, I try to stay positive and learn as much as I can from the situation.
   A. ALWAYS B. MOST OF THE TIME C. SELDOM D. NEVER

4. I've had trials in my life that I wasn't certain I could overcome.
   A. YES, MANY TIMES B. YES, A FEW TIMES C. SELDOM D. NEVER

5. If I see change coming and it's not my idea, I resist it.
   A. I RESIST CHANGE WHETHER IT'S MY IDEA OR NOT.
   B. YES, USUALLY
   C. SOMETIMES
   D. NO. CHANGE IS EXCITING!

6. When my plans fall through, I don't know what to do.
   A. ALWAYS B. MOST OF THE TIME C. SELDOM D. NEVER. I GO TO PLAN B.

7. Sometimes it's good to be flexible, but other times you should stand your ground.
   A. TRUE
   B. FALSE. YOU SHOULD ALWAYS BE FLEXIBLE.
   C. FALSE. YOU SHOULD ALWAYS STAND YOUR GROUND.

8. If people wrong me or hurt my feelings, I can forgive them easily.
   A. YES, ALMOST ALWAYS
   B. YES, SOMETIMES
   C. YES, BUT IT DEPENDS ON WHAT THEY DID.
   D. NOT REALLY, I FOCUS ON PROTECTING MYSELF.

9. When something goes wrong, my initial reaction is to look for who is to blame.
   A. YES, IT'S IMPORTANT TO FIND OUT WHO IS RESPONSIBLE.
   B. OFTEN. I DON'T WANT IT TO BE PINNED ON ME.
   C. SELDOM. THINGS GO WRONG ALL THE TIME.
   D. NO, I TEND TO LOOK FOR SOLUTIONS TO THE PROBLEM.

10. I don't understand why some people will try to do something over and over, even when they fail.
    A. RIGHT! WHAT ARE THEY THINKING?
    B. SOMETIMES YOU NEED TO KNOW WHEN TO GIVE UP.
    C. IT MAKES SENSE AS LONG AS YOU TRY DIFFERENT WAYS.
    D. NEVER GIVE UP. NEVER, NEVER, NEVER.

BUT THOSE WHO TRUST IN THE LORD
WILL RECEIVE NEW STRENGTH.
THEY WILL FLY AS HIGH AS EAGLES.
THEY WILL RUN AND NOT GET TIRED.
THEY WILL WALK AND NOT GROW WEAK.

ISAIAH 40:31

IT'S UP 2 YOU (CONTINUED)

RESILIENCE SCORECARD

1. Answer:	A-5	B-4	C-3	D-2	POINTS:
2. Answer:	A-5	B-4	C-3	D-2	POINTS:
3. Answer:	A-5	B-4	C-3	D-2	POINTS:
4. Answer:	A-5	B-4	C-3	D-2	POINTS:
5. Answer:	A-2	B-3	C-4	D-5	POINTS:
6. Answer:	A-2	B-3	C-4	D-5	POINTS:
7. Answer:	A-5	B-3	C-3		POINTS:
8. Answer:	A-5	B-4	C-3	D-2	POINTS:
9. Answer:	A-2	B-3	C-4	D-5	POINTS:
10. Answer:	A-2	B-3	C-4	D-5	POINTS:

TOTAL POINTS:

RESILIENCE PROFILE

If your total points score was . . .

40–50: Your character is already resilient. You've made mistakes but can honestly say you're a better person because of what you learned from them. You know the value of staying positive and not thinking negatively. When you don't let your circumstances get you down, you gain authority over your circumstances that causes others to look up to you. Rather than blaming others, you're focused on solutions, and may embrace change as a new adventure in life.

30–39: Resilience is a valuable character trait that develops by pressing on when times get hard. Resilience requires taking action and forgiving others. You keep moving even after you fall. Middle school will be difficult for you if you are not resilient. Certainly over the next few years you will be pushed down—it's not a matter of "if" but of "when." Keep pressing forward.

21–29: Whether you're more timid by nature or you've been taught not to take risks, realize that you are overly cautious. Adversity and trials make us stronger; steel is resilient because it has been tempered at very high heat, which gives it the strength to endure great stress. Seek a responsible adult—whether a parent or a mentor—who can encourage you to persevere, to forgive, and to keep moving forward when faced with adversity of any kind.

KINGDOM KEY 15

GOALS

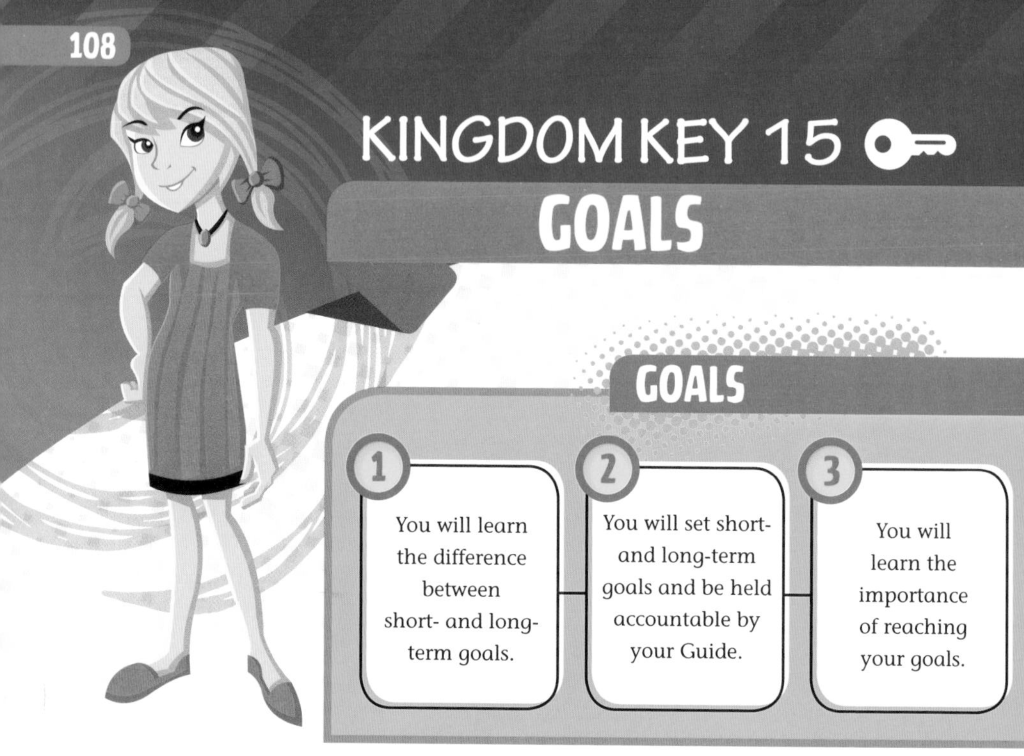

MEANING

Something that you are trying to do or to achieve

GOAL

- **DREAM**—a strongly desired goal or purpose
- **INTENTION**—the thing that you plan to do or achieve; an aim or purpose
- **PLAN**—a set of actions that have been thought of as a way to do or achieve something

Application: You have specific benchmarks and outcomes you aim to achieve, whether they relate to your spiritual, physical, academic, or relational life.

FROM THE WORD

But you, be strong and do not lose courage, for there is reward for your work.
—2 Chronicles 15:7, NASB

DEFINE

What does having a "goal" mean to you?

QUESTIONS 2 PONDER

1. What is the connection between your goals and your purpose?
2. Are long-term goals more important than short-term goals? Explain.
3. Is it okay or dangerous to have unrealistic goals for yourself? Explain.
4. Do you think that someone else can set goals for you?

JUST 4 FUN

1. Go back to the lesson on Identity and rewrite your tagline here. Change it if you need to.

___

___

2. Next, draft a vision statement. Those one or two lines reveal the direction your life is heading—your goals. The vision statement represents you; it shows how you want to present yourself to others. Here are some examples: Make-A-Wish—*Our vision is that people everywhere will share the power of a wish.* Teach for America—*One day, all children in this nation will have the opportunity to attain an excellent education.*

___

___

LONG- AND SHORT-TERM GOALS ACTIVITY

Now it's your turn to come up with three goals. Write down two goals that you want to take place within the next twelve months and one goal to reach before you're twelve years old. Along with each goal, list one to three action steps you can take to reach it. Sign the contract with your Guide so that he or she can hold you accountable along the way.

MY LIFE GOALS

LONG-TERM GOAL #1 FOR THIS YEAR

____

____

____

SHORT-TERM GOALS TO REACH IT

a. ______________________________________

b. ______________________________________

c. ______________________________________

LONG-TERM GOAL #2 FOR THIS YEAR

____

____

____

SHORT-TERM GOALS TO REACH IT

a. ______________________________________

b. ______________________________________

c. ______________________________________

GOAL FOR BEFORE I'M TWELVE

____

____

____

SHORT-TERM GOALS TO REACH IT

a. ______________________________________

b. ______________________________________

c. ______________________________________

________________	________________	________________
MY SIGNATURE	GUIDE'S SIGNATURE	DATE

HERE 2 HELP

As a kingdom kid, the goals you set for the future should be tied to God's purpose and calling on your life. Goals are often discovered by looking at several things, such as

- your passions,
- your gifts,
- your skills,
- your past experiences, and
- your interests.

Oftentimes, these will intersect at some point in your life. Those are exciting moments! You'll gain perspective on why you're here and what you're meant to do and be.

When your goals are clear regarding your future, the decisions you make in the present will relate to those goals. Either your decisions will be directly related to your goals, or they will steer you closer to your goals. You'll have a clear picture of when to say "yes" and when to say "no." You'll have an improved attitude about the things you don't want to do or don't enjoy doing. Why? Because you'll know they will help you reach your goals, and you'll have greater motivation to do them.*

*Adapted from Dr. Tony Evans, *Destiny* (Eugene, OR: Harvest House Publishers, 2012), 87.

WE PLAN THE WAY WE WANT TO LIVE, BUT ONLY GOD MAKES US ABLE TO LIVE IT.

PROVERBS 16:9, MSG

Your vision ought to determine your goals. And your goals ought to determine your actions.

Here's a helpful tool as you establish your goals. Double-check them against this helpful acronym—**SMART**—to make sure these are realistic goals and that you're positioning yourself to reach them:

S—Goals need to be **specific**. This will help you make choices on what to do or not to do in order to reach them.

M—Goals need to be **measurable** in some form or fashion.

A—Goals need to be **attainable**. For example, don't set a goal of being able to kick a football over a mountain—it's impossible. Set yourself up for success rather than failure by choosing goals that are attainable.

R—Goals need to be **relevant**, meaning they should tie into your personal interests or ambitions; otherwise, you may lose interest over time.

T—Goals need to have a **time frame** associated with them. This will keep you on track and not as prone to procrastination as you pursue your goals.

We all can share the goal to live a life of excellence—to work as unto the Lord. We can work with care, productivity, and skill. It means not settling for just getting something finished; it means finishing as well as you can. Living a life of excellence results in choices that keep you in school, instead of dropping out. Excellence gives you a long-range view of your life so that in all you do now, you do it to your highest ability. You do it that way knowing God's Word promises that your work will thrive (2 Chronicles 15:7). All these choices—when grouped together—will get you to the next level so that you can achieve your personal goals.

IT'S UP 2 YOU

Read each statement. Then select the response that best describes your personal experience with goal setting. Circle the corresponding letter. Follow the directions on tallying your score at the end of the quiz. Ask your Guide for help if you have questions.

1. In my family, we set goals together.
   A. YES, AND WE MONITOR OUR PROGRESS.
   B. YES, BUT WE DON'T FOLLOW UP.
   C. WE TALK ABOUT GOALS SOMETIMES.
   D. NO, GOALS AREN'T A TOPIC OF CONVERSATION.

2. I set long-term goals for myself.
   A. FREQUENTLY, AND I REVISIT THEM.
   B. SOMETIMES
   C. SELDOM
   D. VERY RARELY. I LIVE DAY-TO-DAY.

3. I set short-term goals for myself—things that I can accomplish in a day or less.
   A. YES, FREQUENTLY
   B. YES, ESPECIALLY WHEN I HAVE A PROJECT DUE.
   C. SOMETIMES, BUT I SELDOM ACHIEVE THEM.
   D. RARELY OR NEVER

4. My goal, when I am faced with a problem, is to . . .
   A. LEARN AS MUCH AS I CAN SO I CAN HELP OTHERS.
   B. NAVIGATE SAFELY THROUGH IT.
   C. FIND OUT WHO IS TO BLAME FOR THE SITUATION.
   D. TRY TO AVOID TRIALS AT ALL COST.

5. I have a vision for myself in the future, and I'm successful.
   A. YES, MY FUTURE IS BRIGHT.
   B. YES, BUT I'M NOT SURE HOW TO GET THERE.
   C. I HAVEN'T REALLY THOUGHT ABOUT MY FUTURE MUCH.
   D. I SEE ONLY DIMLY.

6. One of my goals in life is to be a disciple of Christ.
   A. YES, I ACTIVELY PURSUE THIS GOAL.
   B. YES, I THINK THIS IS AN IMPORTANT GOAL.
   C. I HAVEN'T GIVEN THIS MUCH THOUGHT AS A GOAL FOR MY LIFE.
   D. I DON'T REALLY HAVE LIFE GOALS.

7. My goal for my friendships right now is . . .
   A. NOT BE ALONE.
   B. HANG WITH PEOPLE WHO THINK AND ACT LIKE I DO.
   C. BE NICE TO OTHERS.
   D. PROMOTE THE WELL-BEING OF OTHERS.

8. I can give myself permission to put my goals on pause.
   A. YES, I OCCASIONALLY DO THIS.
   B. NOT REALLY. I LIKE TO KEEP PRESSING THROUGH TO THE GOAL NO MATTER WHAT.
   C. YES, I DO THIS OFTEN—MAYBE TOO OFTEN.
   D. NO, IF I PAUSE FROM PURSUING A GOAL, I WON'T START AGAIN.

9. Other people help me plan my goals, and I achieve them.
   A. YES, AND I LEARN AND GROW FROM THE PROCESS.
   B. YES, AND I'M NOT TOO EXCITED ABOUT IT.
   C. SELDOM OR NEVER—I WISH THEY WOULD.
   D. THEY USED TO, BUT THEY'VE GIVEN UP ON TRYING TO MAKE ME DO THINGS I DON'T WANT TO DO.

10. My parent(s) support the goals I have for my life.
    A. STRONGLY DISAGREE; I DON'T HAVE ANYONE TO GUIDE ME TOWARD MY GOALS.
    B. DISAGREE; BUT I HAVE ANOTHER ADULT IN MY LIFE WHO DOES SUPPORT ME THROUGH ENCOURAGEMENT AND MENTORING.
    C. AGREE; THEY ENCOURAGE ME AND WE TALK ABOUT MY PROGRESS.
    D. STRONGLY AGREE; THEY HELP ME PLAN AND SET GOALS.

IT'S UP 2 YOU (CONTINUED)

GOALS SCORECARD

1. Answer:	A-5	B-4	C-3	D-2	POINTS:
2. Answer:	A-5	B-4	C-3	D-2	POINTS:
3. Answer:	A-5	B-4	C-3	D-2	POINTS:
4. Answer:	A-5	B-4	C-3	D-2	POINTS:
5. Answer:	A-5	B-4	C-3	D-2	POINTS:
6. Answer:	A-5	B-4	C-3	D-2	POINTS:
7. Answer:	A-2	B-3	C-4	D-5	POINTS:
8. Answer:	A-5	B-4	C-3	D-2	POINTS:
9. Answer:	A-5	B-4	C-3	D-2	POINTS:
10. Answer:	A-2	B-3	C-4	D-5	POINTS:

TOTAL POINTS:

GOALS PROFILE

If your total points score was . . .

40–50: You're a goal setter! You have already organized a path for your life that can enable you to achieve great things. Now you need to set goals to help further the kingdom of God. Be grateful for a parent or other adult in your life who has taught you to set goals and who helps you to accomplish goals toward your vision. Be sure to stay prayerful and in God's Word for changes in direction He may give you along the way.

30–39: Somewhere along the way, you've been taught that goals are important, but you may lack the support or initiative to set goals, self-check your progress, and press toward the prize (Philippians 3:14). You need to prioritize goal setting. That means giving time, energy, thought, and prayer to discovering who you are. That includes your passions, God-given gifts, and talents. You can find a kingdom purpose for your life that brings you joy and is a blessing to other people.

20–29: There is no time like the present to ask yourself, *Who am I and why am I here?* You were made on purpose, for a purpose, by a loving God who has a plan for your life. That plan will unfold as you spend time with Him in prayer and as you begin serving others. Take advantage of the resources around you—your school library's Internet connection, the school counselor, or resources at your school—to learn about options for your future. Engage in conversations with a teacher, mentor, parent, or grandparent whom you admire and trust. He or she will help you stay on track with short- and long-term goals. When learning to be a goal-setter, start small and short-term and then build to the large, long-term goals. Break those long-term goals down into do-able, measurable parts. You can do all things through Christ, who strengthens you (Philippians 4:13).

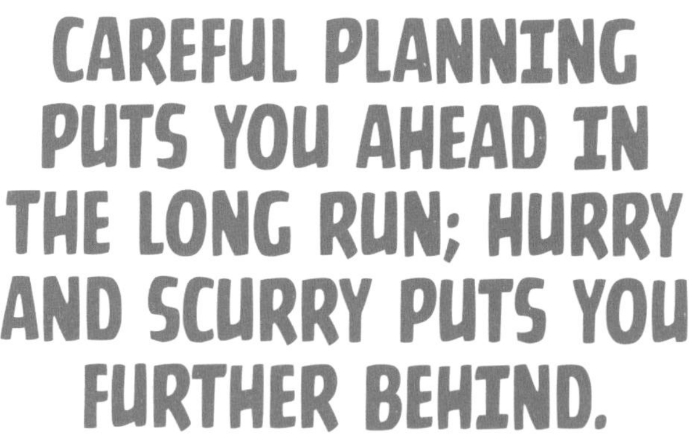

CAREFUL PLANNING PUTS YOU AHEAD IN THE LONG RUN; HURRY AND SCURRY PUTS YOU FURTHER BEHIND.

PROVERBS 21:5, MSG

APPENDIX A: THE ROMANS ROAD

How to Make Sure You're on Your Way to Heaven

The outline I'm using is not original. I didn't discover it; I simply expanded it. However, I've found it simple to remember and easy to use. By using key passages from the book of Romans, we can outline everything a person needs to know in order to receive salvation in Jesus Christ. This content is a little difficult. Be sure your Guide reads it with you in case you have questions.

Let's begin.

Tony Evans

The Problem

For all have sinned and fall short of the glory of God.
—Romans 3:23, NIV

Salvation is *good* news, but it comes to us against a backdrop of *bad* news. The bad news is this: We are all sinners. Not one person on planet Earth—past, present, or future—is without sin.

The Greek word for *sin* means to "miss the mark."* It describes an archer who draws back his string, releases his arrow, but fails to hit the bull's-eye. Similarly, sin involves missing the target. What is the target? The verse we just looked at tells us: "All have sinned and *fall short of the glory of God.*" Sin is falling short of God's glory—His standard.

To help you understand this concept, I must attack a popular myth. The fable is that sin can be measured by degree. For many of us, criminals seem like big-time sinners, while those of us who tell little white lies are lightweight sinners. It appears logical to believe that those sitting in the principal's office have not sinned as seriously as those living in the state prison. But sin looks quite different from God's perspective.

In Scripture, sin is not measured by degree. Either we miss the mark or we don't. Since the entire sin question pivots on this point, let's make sure we understand our target.

The story is told of two men who explored an island when, suddenly, a volcano erupted. In moments, the two found themselves surrounded by molten lava. Several feet away there was a clearing—and a path to safety.

* *Strong's Concordance*, s.v. H264 "*hamartanó*," http://biblehub.com/greek/264.htm.

To get there, however, they'd have to jump across the river of melted rock. The first gentleman was an active senior citizen but hardly an outstanding physical specimen. He ran as fast as he could, took an admirable leap, but traveled only a few feet. He met a swift death in the superheated lava.

The other explorer was a much younger man in excellent physical condition. In fact, the college record he set in the broad jump had remained unbroken to that day. He put all his energy into his run, jumped with flawless form, and shattered his own college record. Unfortunately, he landed far short of the clearing. Though the younger man clearly outperformed his companion, both wound up equally dead. Survival was so far out of reach that ability didn't matter at all.

Degrees of "goodness" may be important when hiring an employee or choosing friends. But when the issue is sin, the only standard that matters is God's perfect holiness. The question is not how we measure up against the kid down the street, but how we measure up to God. God's standard is perfect righteousness, and it's a standard that even the best-behaved or moral person can't reach.

The Penalty

> Sin entered the world through one man, and death through sin, and in this way death came to all men, because all sinned. —**Romans 5:12**, NIV

Now, as you read this passage, you may be thinking, "If sin entered the world through one man (Adam), it isn't fair to punish the rest of us." Yet, death spread to all men because "all have sinned." We are not punished simply because Adam sinned, but because we inherited Adam's tendency to sin, and have sinned ourselves.

Have you ever noticed that you don't need to teach children how to sin? Can you imagine sitting down with a child and saying, "Here's how to lie successfully" or "Let me show you how to be selfish"? Those things come naturally.

Have you ever seen an apple with a small hole in it? If you do, you might not want to eat it. The hole tells you that there was once a worm in there. Now, most people don't know how the worm managed to take up residence in that apple. They think he slithered by one day and then he decided to bore through the outer skin of the fruit and set up house inside. However, that is not what happens. Worms hatch from larvae dropped on the apple blossom. The blossom becomes a bud and the bud turns into fruit. The apple literally grows up around the unborn worm. The hole is left when the worm hatches and digs his way out.

In the same way, the seed of sin is within each and every one of us at the moment of birth. Though it may take some time before evidence of sin shows on the surface, it's there and eventually makes its presence known.

Sin demands a penalty. That penalty, according to Scripture, is death. That means physical death (where the soul is separated from the body) and spiritual death (where the soul is separated from God).

The Provision

> But God demonstrates his own love for us in this: While we were still sinners, Christ died for us. —**Romans 5:8, NIV**

Two very powerful words when put together are "but God." Those words can revolutionize any situation. "My parents are getting a divorce. But God . . ." "My dad lost his job. But God . . ." "I have no friends. But God . . ." God can restore any situation. He is bigger and more powerful than any life challenge or any predicament with or resulting from sin.

"I'm a sinner sentenced to be apart from God. But God . . ." Those same words sum up the Good News for each of us. Even while we were still sinners, God proved His love for us by sending Jesus Christ to die in our place.

How amazing that God would love us so deeply. We have certainly done nothing to deserve it. But the amazement deepens when we consider Jesus' sacrifice on the cross.

You see, we all have sinned, and not just anybody could die for the penalty of sin. We each have our own price to pay. Whoever would save us must be perfectly sinless.

Two brothers were playing in the woods one summer day when almost without warning, a bee flew down and stung the older brother on the eyelid. He put his hands to his face and fell to the ground in pain. As the younger brother looked on in horror, the bee began buzzing around his head. Terrified, he began screaming, "The bee's going to get me!" The older brother, regaining his composure, said, "What are you talking about? That bee can't hurt you, he already stung me."

The Bible tells us that this is precisely what happened on the cross when Jesus died. God loves you so much that He stepped out of heaven in the person of Jesus Christ and took the "stinger of death" in your place. Jesus hung on the cross, not for His own sin, but for my sin and yours. Because He was without sin, His death paid the penalty for all of us.

How do we know that Jesus' death on the cross really took care of the sin problem? Because of what happened on that Sunday morning. When Mary Magdalene came to Jesus' tomb that morning, she couldn't find Him. She saw someone and, thinking it was a gardener, she asked Him where the Lord's body had been taken. When the gardener turned and removed His cloak, Mary gasped in amazement. It was Jesus. And not only did Mary see Him, according to 1 Corinthians, but also more than five hundred people personally saw the risen Christ before He ascended into heaven.

I am a Christian today because the tomb is empty. If not for the Resurrection, our faith would be empty and useless. As the apostle Paul said, if Jesus were not raised, we should be the most pitied people on earth (1 Corinthians 15:14-17). But the fact is, Jesus *is* raised. Now what do we do?

The Pardon

> If you confess with your mouth, "Jesus is Lord," and believe in your heart that God raised him from the dead, you will be saved. For it is with your heart that you believe and are justified, and it is with your mouth that you confess and are saved. —**Romans 10:9-10**, NIV

If good works could save anyone, there would be no point in Jesus' death. But He knew we couldn't pay sin's price. That's why His sacrifice was so important. In order for His sacrifice to secure our pardon, we must trust in Him for our salvation.

Believing *in* Jesus means a great deal more than believing *about* Him. Knowing the facts about His life and death is only head knowledge. Believing in Him demands that we put that knowledge to work. It means to trust, to have total confidence, to "rest your case" on Him. Without knowing, you illustrate this concept every time you sit down. The moment you commit your weight to a chair, you have "believed in" that chair to hold you up. Most of us have so much faith in chairs that, despite our weight, we will readily place ourselves down without a second thought.

You must understand that if you depend on anything beyond Jesus to save you, then what you're really saying is that Jesus Christ is not enough. God is waiting for you to commit the entire weight of your existence to Jesus Christ and what He did on the cross. Your complete eternal destiny must rest upon Him. You must place absolute confidence in the work of Christ alone.

Where Do I Go from Here?

Have you ever confessed your sin to God and trusted in Jesus Christ alone for your salvation? If not, there's no better time than right now.

It all begins with a simple prayer. The exact wording isn't important. What matters is that you mean it. Here's an example:

> *Dear Jesus, I confess that I am a sinner. I deserve the punishment that results from sin. Jesus, I believe that You are holy and sinless, that You died on the cross at Calvary and rose from the dead to give salvation. I now place all my confidence in You as my Savior. Please forgive me of my sins and grant me eternal life. Thank You for saving me. I want to live my life for You. Amen.*

If you prayed that prayer for the first time, I want to welcome you into the family of God. Also, talk with your pastor, your Guide, your parents, and a Christian friend. Let them all know about your decision so they can encourage you and help you to grow in your newfound faith.

APPENDIX B: WHAT IS YOUR PERSONALITY LIKE?

This short quiz isn't a real test that a psychologist or a school counselor would use, but it's fun and can help you understand yourself and others. Here's how it works: Circle fifteen phrases that really, truly sound just like you. Then go to the following chart.

I like to be in charge.

I like to finish what I start.

I like to do the same things in the same way.

I don't often cry or shout.

I talk A LOT!

I don't like to argue.

I'm not afraid to ask for what I want.

People like to do things with me.

People tell me I'm shy.

I like to have a lot of friends.

I like to be noticed.

I like to take care of people.

I'm a good listener.

My teacher says I'm creative.

I like logic puzzles or games.

People seem to like my ideas.

I am a loyal friend.

I have new ideas all the time.

My desk at school is neat and tidy.

My school papers are messy.

I don't agree with everybody.

I often forget to do my homework and chores.

I like to try new things.

I like to know what's right and what's wrong.

I don't like to change my bedroom.

I am curious and like to find answers to my questions.

I like to win at just about everything.

I am usually on time.

I know things will always turn out right.

I like to have fun.

I am patient and thoughtful.

I like just one or two friends.

I take a lot of care with my math papers.

What Animals Are You Like?

These fun animal profiles will help you remember your personality traits. Count how many blue answers your circled. Then red, brown, and green. Fill in the numbers in the chart. (The total should add up to fifteen.) The color with the highest number is your main personality. Read the animal profile that corresponds to that color. If another color is the same or within one point, read that animal description too.

BLUE	RED	BROWN	GREEN

BLUE = ELEPHANT. This personality is "big"—but not the physical size; some elephants are tiny people. You can hardly miss this person—you know when he/she is in the room! Elephants don't mind conflict, so they will say what is on their mind, just like an elephant calls in the wild. Elephants like to win at games and strive to be the best. Elephants don't always notice others, and so they can accidentally "squash" them. Elephants are good leaders because they're brave and strong enough to clear a path for others.

RED = ANT. If an elephant is a "big" personality, the ant is a "small" personality. Ants don't show their emotions, and others think of them as shy. Often they have clean desks, clean clothes, and clean bedrooms. It's important for ants to know the rules of a game or the classroom. What's right and what's wrong matter to them. Like real ants that carry food to the anthill, people with an ant personality start what they finish. Ants also make plans. Just as real ants have elaborate anthills, people with this personality trait think through hard problems, and they work hard on a project till it's done—and done well.

BROWN = PUPPY. A puppy loves company and everyone loves a puppy! Puppies talk a lot and make others feel comfortable. They may leave a messy room or desk at school in the same way a young dog messes up a house with its toys. Puppies look to have fun, and so doing homework or chores seems burdensome. They are positive, creative, and full of great ideas.

GREEN = PONY. Ponies are loyal to one or two people. They like it when everyone is happy, and so they don't argue. In the same way a real pony is comfortable taking the same trail every day, a person with a pony personality likes to do things in the same way. Ponies' quiet nature makes them good listeners. Like a real pony that carries a rider, people with pony personalities like to help others.

*This quiz was developed by Marianne Hering.